PRAISE FOR ODDS-ON BASKET

M000250552

"There are two books that I would recommend John Wooden's *Practical Modern Basketball* a *Basketball Coaching*, which focuses on crafting ...., game situations to increase your team's success. Coffino's book is loaded with knowledge on how to be a better coach. I wish he had published it while I was still coaching because it would have been a real asset."—Dale Brown, head men's basketball coach, Louisiana State University (1972–1997), and member of the College Basketball Coaches Hall of Fame

"Coaches at every level can learn from *Odds-On Basketball Coaching*. It is as comprehensive and fresh an approach to game situations as you will find."—Jennifer Azzi, head women's basketball coach, University of San Francisco (2010–2016), member of the Women's Basketball Hall of Fame, Olympic gold medal winner, and former WNBA player

"*Odds-On Basketball Coaching* is chock-full of coaching goodies like none I've ever read, challenging coaches to think deeply and differently about game situations. I only wish my coaching staffs and I had the book all my previous coaching years. Especially with modern technology, it can be used effectively in a wide range of innovative ways."—Jeff Ruland, two-time NBA All-Star and assist leader, NBA Development League head coach, and 13-year Division I college coach (4 NCAA appearances)

"*Odds-On Basketball Coaching* is valuable for all coaches regardless of experience or coaching level. It challenges you to think and reflect on your entire approach to coaching while giving you new insight into the game of basketball."—Sara Lee, head women's basketball coach, Dennison University

"*Odds-On Basketball Coaching* is a well thought out and comprehensive guide that would be helpful to young coaches. It allows the coach to think through each situation presented and consider which of several strategies should be employed. The added bonus is that you get to do this before the added pressure of the game. A good read and a great way to prepare for the upcoming season."—Bret Tovani, head men's basketball coach, Dominican College (2005–2011) and head boys' varsity basketball coach, San Rafael High School and the Branson School, 33 combined years

"*Odds-On Basketball Coaching* is a great read. Game management, situations, and coaching philosophy is not talked about or practiced enough at the high school level. This book planted seeds that will make me a better coach next season and in years to come. Coach Coffino's book is one I will reference many times in the future to prepare our team for any in-game situation that may arise."—Steve Campagno, head boys' varsity basketball coach, Redwood High School (2008–present)

"ALL coaches, especially on the high school level, need to read this book. It is a comprehensive resource on most every conceivable situational play that a team may encounter. As significantly, this book serves as a tremendous reminder that we coaches need to carve out substantial practice time for preparing our players on precisely what our team WILL encounter during a given season."—Chris Lavdiotis, head boys' varsity basketball coach, Piedmont High School (2001–present)

"Coach Coffino's attention to detail in all facets of the game is a must read for coaches at all levels. *Odds-On Basketball Coaching* is organized in a way to find ideas and solutions for any situation. A great tool and reference guide."—Mike Saia, head boys' varsity basketball coach, Marin Catholic High School, and former NCAA basketball referee

ODDS-ON BASKETBALL COACHING

Crafting High-Percentage Strategies for Game Situations

Michael J. Coffino

ROWMAN & LITTLEFIELD
Lanham • Boulder • New York • London

Published by Rowman & Littlefield
A wholly owned subsidiary of The Rowman & Littlefield Publishing Group,
Inc.
4501 Forbes Boulevard, Suite 200, Lanham, Maryland 20706
www.rowman.com

Unit A, Whitacre Mews, 26-34 Stannary Street, London SE11 4AB

British Library Cataloguing in Publication Information Available

Library of Congress Cataloging-in-Publication Data

Names: Coffino, Michael, author.
Title: Odds-On Basketball Coaching : Crafting High-Percentage Strategies for Game Situations /
Michael J. Coffino.
Description: Lanham : Rowman & Littlefield, [2017] | Includes index.
Identifiers: LCCN 2016056495 (print) | LCCN 2017001412 (ebook) | ISBN 9781538101964 (hard-
cover : alk. paper) | ISBN 9781538101971 (pbk. : alk. paper) | ISBN 9781538101988 (electronic)
Subjects: LCSH: Basketball—Coaching. | Basketball—Training. | Basketball—Psychological as-
pects.
Classification: LCC GV885.3 C638 2017 (print) | LCC GV885.3 (ebook) | DDC 796.32307/7—
dc23
LC record available at https://lccn.loc.gov/2016056495

Printed in the United States of America

To my sons, coaches Torin Coffino and Aidan Coffino, my reality checkers and basketball muses, whose brilliant basketball minds and infectious passion for the game inspire me every day.

CONTENTS

ACKNOWLEDGMENTS

I am forever grateful for the support and guidance of my brother, coach John Coffino, whose encyclopedic basketball mind produced countless insights and perspectives for this book, and who, to borrow a cliché, has likely forgotten more about the game than I can ever know. I cannot overstate the value of his contributions and unwavering encouragement.

My son Aidan Coffino, an enormously talented basketball coach in his own right, gave me keen editorial contributions on content and style throughout the project and, as always, injected me with reality checks every step of the way.

Thank you coach Bill Washauer, my loyal and trusted varsity assistant coach and sounding board for three years of high school hoops, for taking the time to peruse and comment on the first draft of the manuscript. As with everything he does, his contributions were first-rate.

Every writer should be so lucky to have a friend with the boundless writing talent and generosity of spirit of Steve Yafa to guide and advise them during their writing projects. I count myself among the lucky ones to have regular access to such an incisive mind. A bow of gratitude and thanks.

Thank you Robert Stricker, my writing consigliore, who blessed me with his timeless wisdom throughout the journey of writing this book. His perspectives are priceless.

Thank you Christen Karniski, of Rowman & Littlefield, for believing in this project and for your insights on and contributions to the final product.

And much thanks to Joan Barnes, whose creative brilliance is unmatched and whose reservoir of ideas overflows constantly.

PREFACE

"If you try to fail, and succeed, which have you done?"—George Carlin

With two seconds left in the game, we are down two and at the line shooting two, the climactic moment of a feverish second-half comeback. Given the deep hole we have climbed out of, we look good. The home crowd is anxiously anticipating an overtime frame.

Not so fast. We miss the front-end shot, taking a large gulp of air out of the heroic-moment bag. I call timeout. We have one option: miss the foul shot intentionally and, in less than two seconds, convert the rebound and force overtime. A Herculean task in the best of circumstances, it is now more difficult because we have neither practiced nor been in this situation. We are in uncharted and turbulent waters.

I ask the anxious foul shooter to take a deep breath, hold it for a moment, and let the air out slowly. As he does, I mimic the breathing exercise to provide support and create focus for everyone in the huddle. I smile and say, "Okay, here is what we need to do. First, you are going to shoot the ball immediately after the referee hands it to you. Do not start your foul-shooting routine. Do not wait for anything. When he hands you the ball, the defense will not be set. They will be standing around the lane. They will not be ready."

I repeat this in a slightly different way:

"Understand, as soon as you have the ball, shoot it. At that moment, the other team will not be ready; they will be standing around on the lane line. Okay?"

I raise my eyebrows and look my player in the eye, searching for evidence of comprehension. He nods his head. I wonder if I am getting through. But with no time to stress, I continue.

"Next, shoot the ball directly off the front rim so it comes right back to you, like making a chest pass off a flat wall. This is important. You must hit the front rim as near to the center as you can. You want the ball to come right back to you, like a boomerang. Okay?"

He nods again.

"The ball should come straight back to you. Grab it and, with a single dribble, take one long step down the middle toward the basket and lay it over the rim into the cup. Do everything like that and we get to play four more minutes. Okay?"

He looks at me and says, "Yes, coach."

We break huddle, and he walks slowly to the line. As soon as the referee gives him the ball, he does precisely what I instructed. He lets it loose before the defense has a clue, and sure enough, the ball comes directly back to him off one bounce. He grabs the ball, takes one dribble in a single motion, and lays the damn thing in the basket before the buzzer sounds. The instantaneous roar from the crowd in the packed gym is deafening.

The execution was perfect, save one minor detail: The ball never hit the rim. He shot it down the middle, as directed, but it traveled in a straight line over—and narrowly missing—the front rim and caromed off the glass, coming directly back to him—like making a chest pass off a flat wall. Because the missed shot did not draw iron, it was a rule violation, nullifying the buzzer-beating basket.

The game is over, and we have lost by two.

Later that night, and for much of the next day, I did what most coaches do following such a loss: I obsessed about a litany of "what ifs." I had to acknowledge that had we practiced such an end-of-the-game situation, we likely would have gone into overtime. As it was, I asked a player, in a stressful situation, in front of a standing-room-only crowd, to execute a play he had never performed—a play that required precise execution. While he could have made the first foul shot and avoided the predicament, I felt this one was largely on me. I had not prepared the team for that moment.

I also knew that while we had worked on game situations in practice, we didn't do so nearly enough. I suspected most coaches were in the same boat. I began to jot down as many situations as I could recall where I had been the coach, as well as any others that came to mind. After making the list, I roughly calculated the percentage of those situations I had worked on in practice. The percentage was embarrassingly low. I then informally polled fellow coaches and anecdotally found similar results. The other coaches also spend the vast majority of practice time on fundamentals, conditioning, skill development, offensive and defensive systems, and scrimmages, bemoaning the fact that they barely have enough time for those activities.

I decided something was wrong with this picture. As coaches, we are duty-bound to prepare players for game competition. And while we prepare them in various ways, we devote relatively little time to priming them for the specific situations they tend to see. How do you, for example, make maximum use of the possessions likely left at a certain points of crunch time to increase chances for success? What adjustments should be made to launch a comeback in particular circumstances? What are the various ways to use dead-ball moments for maximum advantage? When up by three points with only several seconds left in a game and playing defense, do the probabilities of success favor fouling to take away the three-point shot or taking chances on straight-up defense? When do the probabilities favor purposefully missing foul shots, and how do you execute on the miss?

I had read books, articles, and blogs about basketball situations, and while helpful, they were not comprehensive and did not offer a framework for making preparation for game situations an integral part of a basketball program. The more I thought about it, the more convinced I became that a different kind of book about situational basketball could make a difference in game performance and outcome.

And so I set out to compose a different kind of work on the subject of situational basketball, and what follows is the result.

It may be a simple game, this game we love, but it never stops teaching. I hope this book in some way contributes to how the game is approached and taught.

INTRODUCTION

The Four Ps of Situational Basketball

"The 50–50–90 rule: Anytime you have a 50–50 chance of getting something right, there's a 90 percent probability you'll get it wrong."—Andy Rooney

Situational basketball—a term of art for particular game moments—is where coaches place their mark on game performance and outcome. It is where coaching philosophy is applied in real time and game preparedness has its most specific impact.

This book is intended, more than anything, to stimulate coaches to think more comprehensively and realistically about how to approach common and uncommon game situations. It is also focused on providing a framework for game decisions that goes beyond instincts and habits, inspiring coaches to devote more time to getting players ready for specific situations, especially those that are likely to occur during the normal course of a season.

On the other hand, this book does not provide an exhaustive list of answers to questions about how to handle game situations. While consensus might exist among coaches about how to handle some situations, making decisions during a game is generally a blend of making a judgment about probabilities, personnel assessment, coaching style, experience, and philosophy; in other words, one size does not fit all. For this reason, this book poses nearly as many questions as it provides viewpoints, hoping to provoke coaches to think more critically about the game circumstances they may face and make preparation for game situations a more integral part of their practices.

This book is built around what I call the "Four Ps of Situational Basketball":

1. Philosophy
2. Practice
3. Personnel
4. Probabilities

The four Ps of situational basketball are interwoven. Your *philosophy*, a blend of style and experience, provides a framework for what you prioritize and emphasize in *practice* and how you use your *personnel*, including coaching staff, to fill the different roles for efficient and effective game performance. Assessment of the *probabilities* allows coaches to more effectively apply their *philosophy*, use their *personnel*, and run their *practices* to make well-considered game decisions.

PHILOSOPHY

Coaches each have a coaching philosophy, embodied in principles, rules, habits, and style of play that define the uniqueness of a basketball program. It is, at base, a value system of what you hold important, including how you prioritize preparation for game competition, create team expectations, and allocate responsibility for the different game roles.

PRACTICE

Game outcomes often turn on a limited number of possessions. Three or four possessions are often the difference in games decided by fewer than 10 points. This means a single possession each quarter in high school and two per half in college. And many of these possessions present situations that recur, sometimes week to week.

A saying that can be traced to former Boston Celtics head coach Doc Rivers speaks to the power of positivity and preparation, and applies with force to special situations: "Be there before you get there." As the story goes, Rivers, without disclosing destination or purpose, took his players on a sojourn through Boston before the start of the season. The itinerary was the route through the city the parade would follow if the Celtics won the NBA title. He wanted them to envision the joy of winning it all before doing so.

In addition to know-how, players need a comfort level, born of familiarity, to feel adept at handling game situations before they face them. Players' confidence in pressure situations is stronger when they have seen them in practice, especially if the rigor in practice exceeds game challenges. Expecting players to handle special game situations effectively without practicing them is not realistic. Players simply perform better in familiar situations, as repetition builds sound habits and comfort levels.

The late Dick DeVenzio, founder of Point Guard College, aptly noted, "Basketball is a thinking game, but, as a coach, one of your major responsibilities is to take as many situations as possible out of thought processes and turn them into quick reactions requiring no thought at all."

Coaches need the same degree of familiarity. Emotional moments strain our ability to think clearly and decisively. The more we prepare for game moments, the easier it is to handle them. A thoughtfully developed system for special situations removes much of the guesswork and unnecessary stress from making decisions in heated moments during a game. Says coach George Raveling, "More games are won during practice than during the game itself."

PERSONNEL

Knowing your personnel (KYP) is an integral part of being an effective coach. Coaches appropriately start each season with hope and a vision. We want our players to succeed, however we define success, and over-achieve, if possible. We also sometimes get locked into how we believe players *should* perform and lose sight of what we realistically can expect of them. Our hopes can spawn expectations that outpace what our players can realistically produce.

Teams are well served if coaches tailor the contours and details of game strategy to fit their players using an honest assessment of their capabilities. Knowing our personnel allows us to account for their limitations and define specific game roles for which they are best suited. Common situations can call for different strategies based on the abilities of your personnel. Asking players to do more than their skill sets and temperaments can provide can tax their ability to succeed and, even worse, doom them to failure.

The same dose of realism applies to the allocation of responsibilities among the coaching staff, especially in games. There is too much distraction, energy, and pressure for a head coach to account for every possible idea and adjustment in game situations. Head coaches need help, especially down the stretch in tough games. Wisely organizing the roles of the coaching staff minimizes angst and hasty decision making when it matters most.

PROBABILITY

Most game decisions, particularly adjustments, seek to improve the probability for success. Indeed, a persuasive argument exists that each decision a coach makes during a game has an element of playing the odds, whether done consciously or subconsciously. For example, coaches who direct players to foul a poor free-throw shooter when in catchup mode assume that the player will fare worse at the line than a teammate with a better free-throw history. A coach who, in the waning seconds of a game when leading by three, fouls purposely to take away the three-point shot assumes that a fouling strategy is more likely to produce a win than defending straight up and risking a three-point shot. When coaches place more ball handlers in the game to deal with a pressure defense, they assume that the new unit is less likely to turn the ball over than the substituted group. A coach who allows an initially shaky substitute to stay in the game is playing the odds the player will settle down and perform more effectively. The examples are endless.

While we coaches sometimes think in terms of "probabilities"—for instance, fouling a poor foul shooter purposely—we tend not to do so in a systematic way. We often act on instinct or out of habit. While it is true that instinct and habit are honed from experience and give us an inherent sense of the probabilities in particular situations, the more consciously we think about probabilities and weigh relevant factors, the better the odds decisions can yield improved results. Application of the four Ps of situational basketball provides a framework for developing a system that increases the odds of achieving success in games. Late San Francisco 49ers Coach Bill Walsh once said, "A resolute and resourceful leader understands that there are a multitude of means to increase the probability of success. And that's what it all comes down to, namely, intelligently and relentlessly seeking solutions that will increase your chance of prevailing in a competitive environment."

I

TIMEOUTS

Mom to six-year-old: "I have had enough. You are getting a timeout."
Six-year-old to mom: "Will that be a full or a 30, mom?"

Tonight we face a team that matches up well with us, and I am
without an assistant. I have to scramble to stay on top of everything
and, at one point, forget to remind the players the possession arrow
favors us, meaning we do not need to burn a timeout to save a
possession if we grapple over a loose ball. As luck has it, there is a
loose ball on the floor when we have the possession arrow. As we
gain possession on the floor, the other team descends rugby style on
our player, who instinctively calls timeout. I give myself a figurative
kick in the ass. While the possession arrow stays with us, we burn a
timeout unnecessarily.

The game is back and forth the entire way, with several strategic
moments, and I use timeouts more than usual, mindful that I am
risking closing the game armed with fewer timeouts than I normally
prefer. With 20 seconds to go in the game, the other team takes a
two-point lead. I call timeout—my final one—to set up a play. Normally, in this situation, I have at least another timeout for an emer-
gency, for example, if we have difficulty inbounding the ball. I call a
play that has our point guard create off penetration. It starts out well
enough, but after he penetrates and dishes, the defense traps the ball
on the catch. I instinctively being to raise my hands to form the T to
save the pass receiver, and as I do, I realize I have no timeouts left.
Down come the hands, and I am left to watch in slow motion as we

suffer a five-second call. We lose the possession, have to foul immediately, and lose by four.

TIMEOUT PHILOSOPHY

Like any part of the game, the thoughtful use of timeouts provides
advantages and can, in the right situation, determine games. To begin,
do you have a coaching philosophy for the use of timeouts? Are you, for
example, disinclined to use them, preferring that your athletes figure
things out for themselves and, in the process, reap the long-term benefits? If so, you are in good company, as some renowned coaches—John
Wooden, Dean Smith, and Phil Jackson come to mind—have had similar philosophies. In contrast, is your approach more structured, whereas
you prefer to save a minimum number of timeouts for the end of the
game? Or is your philosophy game-specific, where you play each game
by ear? Do you prefer to use the shorter timeouts first, saving the
longer ones for later in the game?

These questions, no matter what the answers, help formulate a well-
considered philosophy for the use of timeouts in games. Players and
coaching staff should be in tune with your timeout philosophy so game
expectations are formed accordingly.

RULES AND ROLES

A set of rules and defined roles regarding timeouts enhances efficiency
and helps avoid confusion. This is especially true for tracking timeouts,
establishing team routines during timeouts, vesting authority to call
timeouts, and dealing with referees.

Tracking Timeouts

When practical, an assigned assistant should check with the official
scorer to confirm timeouts remaining for both teams. Official scorers
err sometimes, and the sooner an error is discovered the better the

chances of correction. The same assistant should be responsible for reminding players how many timeouts remain for both teams, particularly in late-game situations, and—this gets ignored a lot—which team has the possession arrow. Knowing which team has the possession arrow informs players about whether they should call timeout in a looming held-ball situation. These things cannot be left to chance.

Timeout Routines

Do you have a routine that players follow for timeouts? For example, do your players stroll or sprint to the bench when a timeout is called? A quick assembly preserves precious seconds and maintains team energy and camaraderie. Furthermore, during a full timeout, some coaches insist that players stay on the floor, while others have the players in the game sit on chairs and face the coach as the rest of the team huddles around. Some schools use a huddle format, with everyone standing with their arms around one another. There are variations. Regardless of your preferences, consistency is important.

Authority to Call a Timeout

In most programs, the head coach is generally the only one who has the authority to signal a timeout. Clarity here increases efficiency and effectiveness, and minimizes the risk that a referee will signal a timeout when the head coach has not called for one. If you want an assistant to have that authority, tell the game officials; otherwise, they might not acknowledge the timeout coming from them.

A more difficult question is when, if ever, to provide players with the discretion to call a timeout on the floor. Consider these situations: (1) you may lose possession because of an impending held ball, (2) a passer is having difficulty inbounding the ball, (3) a defended ball handler is having difficulty advancing the ball, and (4) a player is trapped. Should the players under siege have the prerogative to call a timeout in any or all of these situations? Arguably, that player knows best whether escape options exist. On the other hand, most players probably do not have the big picture of timeout preservation in mind during these moments, at least not the way you do.

Moreover, what if a player is trying to call a timeout and the referees don't see it? Should other players be allowed to call the timeout, for instance, a point guard or other designated player? The gut reaction may be yes, but is that the best approach? Whatever your preference, a possession and a timeout are both at stake, and you want to avoid a last-second decision or no-decision. It is best that these situations be discussed in advance to minimize confusion.

It is also important to consider whether to permit a player to call a timeout to save a ball from going out of bounds. A rule is helpful. For example, consider allowing players to call a timeout in that situation only at certain junctures of the game, for instance, when a minimum amount of time is left in the game (e.g., less than three minutes) or when the team has two or more timeouts remaining.

Communicating with Referees about Timeouts

Communicating with referees about calling timeouts is especially important during crunch time. If you anticipate a timeout, particularly in a loud gym, let the referees know in advance. How many times have you yelled timeout to cement ears? Most coaches, for example, will tell referees they want to call a timeout "on the make" of a foul shot, when things are quieter. The same applies for players on the floor. Take, for instance, the inbounds situation. If the other team is pressing and you anticipate that they will attempt to deny the first pass, have your designated floor spokesperson tell the referees that the team intends to call timeout if needed to avoid a five-second call, if that is what you prefer. A referee who expects the timeout may be less inclined to signal the turnover if the timing is close.

FREE TIMEOUTS

There are many game situations where you can accomplish the same goals as you would with allocated timeouts without actually using the timeout. The coaching staff—and here again assistants play an important role—should be mindful of each opportunity to get information to the team through means other than using a formal timeout, and players too should be schooled in the art of taking advantage of these opportunities. The following is a suggested list:

- *Free Timeout #1 (When a Player Fouls Out).* In high school, a team typically has 20 seconds to identify a substitute for a fouled-out player. This allows the coach to meet with the four remaining players on the floor during the interval. While you should be mindful of applicable rules—most jurisdictions do not permit bench players to join the four on the floor—the opportunity should not be passed up. When the 20 seconds are up, you can talk to the substitute en route to join teammates or have floor leaders update the substitute.
- *Free Timeout #2 (Game Delay).* Another free timeout occurs when a player is injured or a game suffers a delay for other reasons (e.g., a clock malfunction). While the extra time varies with each situation, there is typically ample time to gather players and impart wisdom.
- *Free Timeout #3 (Period Breaks).* All coaches huddle with their teams at the end of the first and third quarters in high school, and these opportunities are self-evident. It is worth noting, however, that this particular stoppage has the quality of starting anew. For that reason, consider striking a positive chord and setting a specific goal for the next period (e.g., holding the other team to a specific number of points).
- *Free Timeout #4 (The Other Team's Timeout).* How often have you geared up to call a timeout when you hear a whistle signaling that your opponent has called one? Consider this a gift. While not always practical, have an assistant track the number of timeouts taken by the other team for this purpose, especially in the fourth quarter, when the other team may be more apt to call timeouts.
- *Free Timeout #5 (Three Shots at the Foul Line).* When a player on either team is at the line with three foul shots, there is ample time to convene a short meeting, whether it be with floor leadership, nonshooters if your player is at the line, or the entire team if the other team is shooting. As many as 20 seconds can be available during the first two shots, a virtual regular timeout.
- *Free Timeout #6 (Substitutions: The Mini Timeout).* Substitutions present opportunities to deliver instructions to players on the

floor. Each time you send a player to the scorer's table to enter the fray, think about arming the substitute with information to share with waiting teammates (e.g., a changed defense or a play for the next possession).

- *Free Timeout #7 (Dead Balls: Without the Coach).* Dead-ball situations are opportunities for players to assemble. Encourage them to do so as much as possible, even if only for a few seconds. These situations include substitutions, held balls, foul calls, or when the ball has gone out of bounds. The team leadership on the floor should be responsible for gathering teammates during these moments, to reaffirm the defense or defensive matchups and rotations, clarify any confusion, provide rebounding reminders, discuss the next offensive possession, or simply rally with encouragement. Said the ever-sagacious Gregg Popovich, "I can't make every decision for you. I don't have 14 timeouts. You guys got to get together and talk."

- *Free Timeout #8 (First Foul Shot: The Other Mini Timeout).* Consider having your team sprint to the bench before the first shot of a two-shot foul to receive quick instructions. If this proves too chaotic or challenging, limit the gathering to your captains or point guard, or to the side of the floor nearest your bench. A similar situation occurs when either team is awarded foul shots because of a technical, which requires all players to move off the foul line.

FORMAL TIMEOUTS

What happens during timeouts differs from coach to coach. Here is one take on how to use this time wisely.

The Short Timeout

For the short, 20- or 30-second timeout, try to focus on only one thing, as time and attention spans are limited. As Leonardo da Vinci once said, "Simplicity is the ultimate sophistication."

The Full Timeout

Divide the full, one-minute timeout into two parts: First, use the initial seconds to allow players to get their wind, hydrate, and clear their heads, while coaches meet and compare notes. Second, during the team meeting part of the timeout, players should pay close attention to the head coach, and only one coach should speak at a time. When one coach is speaking, all eyes should be on that coach. Distractions are plentiful in game situations, and a restated expectation about how players should pay attention is vital. Bear in mind that players tend to remember the last bit of information given before the huddle breaks. In addition, it is more effective to give player-specific instructions after the huddle disbands rather than use the group part of the timeout.

As players begin to exit the huddle and return to the floor, coaches are well advised to remind them of the defense the team is using and other important details applicable to the moment. Finally, be willing to identify moments where you have little helpful to say; otherwise your words will likely fall on deaf ears and do more damage than good. Returning to the wise words of Gregg Popovich,

> Sometimes in timeouts I'll say, "I've got nothing for you. What do you want me to do? We just turned it over six times. Everybody's holding the ball. What else do you want me to do here? Figure it out." And I'll get up and walk away. Because it's true. There's nothing else I can do for them. I can give them some bulls—, and act like I'm a coach or something, but it's on them.

STRATEGIC USES FOR TIMEOUTS

Coaches are not, as a species, reserved, and the specific purposes of timeouts are as varied as what coaches have to say in them. The following is a list of strategic purposes to consider.

- *Breaking the Other Team's Momentum.* Whether and when to burn a timeout to break an opponent's momentum depends, in part, on timeout philosophy, how well you know your personnel, whether it is early or late in the season, how bad the situation has become, what message(s) you want to send to both teams, and how many timeouts you are holding.

- *Changing Game Strategy.* Here, timeouts are as content-filled as they can get. Coaches can address everything from making changes to the defense that jumpstart defensive energy or spring surprises, for example, traps or pressing defenses, to discussing how to handle screens (e.g., from a hedge to a switch), to altering the pace of the game.

- *Relaxing and Motivating Your Team.* If your team is out of sorts and the odds of self-adjustment are not favorable, it is advisable to call a timeout to address the situation. In these moments, players usually know they have fallen off track and do not need a coaching harangue. Instead, they need a reboot and vote of confidence. Remember, a coach's emotional demeanor and body language belie words to the contrary. Players feed off of coaching energy and tone.

- *Drawing up a Specific Play.* What are the odds your team can effectively execute something new in a game situation? On the one hand, a new (and thus unscouted) play can induce surprise and provide an advantage. On the other hand, drawing up something entirely new is risky. Players generally need to practice new plays for an appreciable period of time to be able to execute them effectively, and drawing up something new can waste the timeout. Again, know your personnel and gauge the probabilities. It is better, perhaps, to use a counter of a known play, a minor adjustment that is easier to execute and retains the element of surprise. If you use a set play, consider having a player outline it on a clipboard during the timeout to create better focus.

- *Icing a Free-Throw Shooter.* While some coaches are skeptical about this strategy, especially because it gives the other team a "free" timeout, it can be effective in a tight game, especially with a relatively poor free-throw shooter on the line. Again, you should assess the odds that the timeout will provide the extra rattle effect you want.

- *Instructing on Specific Plays or Defenses Not Being Executed Properly.* Sometimes you have to collect your players to remind them of what they are doing incorrectly, especially if a pattern has developed. It is better to try to correct the flaw than allow a developing negative pattern to become a bad habit.

- *Giving Your Players a Rest.* This especially applies when playing up-tempo teams or teams that press, and when the bench is relatively thin for whatever reason.
- *Preparing for the Final Minutes of a Close Game.* When should you spend a timeout to review game-ending strategy? To some extent, it depends on how much you trust your personnel to make good decisions down the stretch. Regardless, reminders can be helpful, even decisive, especially if you have timeouts to use.
- *Preparing for a Final Possession of a Period or the Game.* In this classic timeout situation, the goal is to focus each player narrowly on what to do in a single possession.
- *Substituting Players.* It is sometimes necessary to call a timeout to substitute players rather than wait for the next dead-ball moment. (See chapter 3 for a more in-depth discussion of this type of timeout.)
- *Getting a Player in Foul Trouble off the Floor.* When, if ever, should you use a timeout to get a player in foul trouble off the floor? Ideally, you want to wait for the whistle after a dead ball. But if the wait lingers, you may have to burn the timeout.
- *Calling a Timeout When None Are Left.* While this scenario is obviously rare, it can be advisable to call a timeout you do not have (and suffer the corresponding technical) when there is sufficient time in the game to implement something you believe is crucial. If you take this unusual step, try to call the timeout during a dead-ball situation to avoid losing an active possession. It can also be useful in a game you have effectively won or lost and want to get bench players on the floor.
- *Calling Back-to-Back Timeouts.* While it is also rare to call back-to-back timeouts, why hesitate to call the second timeout if there is a compelling need for more time with your players and you can afford to burn another? When the chips are on the line, philosophy and pride account for little.

PLAYING WITH NO TIMEOUTS

While the need to play with no timeouts remaining hopefully does not occur with any regularity, it does happen, as the opening scenario to this chapter shows. For starters, you probably cannot remind your team enough that you are out of timeouts. The most infamous illegal timeout occurred when Michigan, out of timeouts and down two to North Carolina, called timeout with 11 seconds left in the 1993 NCAA championship game. The timeout resulted in a technical against Michigan, costing them a possession and an opportunity to tie the game, and the horror of two foul shots and possession being awarded to North Carolina. The backstory is that Michigan head coach Steve Fisher, during a preceding timeout (with 46 seconds left in the game), reminded his team they had no further timeouts. But here was the rub. Three more possessions ensued: a turnover by North Carolina; a score by Michigan off a second-chance opportunity after that turnover; and a foul of a North Carolina player, who hit the first and missed the second of two free throws. The rebound on the missed foul shot on that last possession led to the possession during which Michigan called a timeout it did not have. Thus, three possessions occurred between the no-timeout reminder and the fateful moment.

Hindsight, of course, is clear as day. It is easy to say that the Michigan coaching staff should have reminded the team repeatedly they had no timeouts after they took the floor, including when they had the ball before the doomed possession. In fact, in the chaos of the fateful possession, when North Carolina began to trap, players on the Michigan bench feverishly yelled "no timeouts." In the commotion, however, Chris Webber, who called the illicit timeout, instead heard a command to call a timeout. He followed the directions he heard, and the rest is NCAA lore.

The point is not to second-guess the Michigan coaching staff—Fisher justifiably could have taken comfort in his initial reminder about the absence of any timeouts—but to learn a valuable lesson. Particularly in stressful conditions—and the 1993 NCAA championship game was as stressful as they get—players need help from the bench. One reminder may not suffice. The assistant coach in charge of timeouts should constantly remind the team of the timeout situation.

Avoiding the negative consequences of calling a timeout you lack is not the only potential challenge you may have in this situation. More difficult is how you manage the game, especially in the closing moments after you have spent your last timeout. Assume, for example, you need to go full court and score to win or tie. You cannot call timeout. What do you do? Do you have a set play for this situation that you can signal from the bench? Who is your best long passer? Remember, too, that you can use a substitution during a dead-ball situation to have the new player relay instructions to the players on the floor.

What about when the other team has no timeouts? One approach is to place pressure (with one of your bigs) on the inbound passer or try to deny the pass to likely receivers by double-teaming to force a five-second call. Again, practice this situation and give it a name.

What if your team is on the adverse end of that situation? Think about using a loud count of five seconds, either from the bench or from the inbounder. If the count gets to four and you can't call a timeout, rather than turn the ball over and have the ball awarded to the other team under their own basket, throw the ball down the floor looking for a receiver and a possible play. At a minimum, the ball gets stolen or goes out of bounds and you get to set up your defense. This, too, requires practice time for effective execution.

✿ ✿ ✿

There are ample opportunities to impart information to players throughout the course of a game, whether during lulls in the action or official timeouts. These moments should be cherished. The collective opportunity this presents to improve the chances for success is immeasurable and cannot be left solely to game instinct and style, but should be carefully honed and planned and the subject of routines for players and coaches to honor. Furthermore, using all available opportunities to speak with the team and for players to speak with one another has an important residual benefit: It enhances team cohesion, builds relationships, and improves the valued skill of effective communication.

2

FOUL SITUATIONS

"We're shooting 100 percent: 60 percent from the field and 40 percent from the free-throw line."—Norm Stewart

The game is tied, 29–29, with 19 seconds left in the first half. Two minutes ago, we were up, 27–22. The other team, however, rattled off seven straight to grab its first lead before we finally scored a moment ago to knot the game at 29. We have lost well-earned momentum. As the ball drops through the net on our game-tying make, I call timeout. We have only four team fouls and can burn two, risk-free. I substitute two players who can afford fouls and explain that I want to give the first foul at 10 to 12 seconds left in the half and the second with about eight seconds left. I remind them how we have practiced this situation: When the other team shoots, we will leak the topside guard looking for a baseball pass and transition opportunity. I remind an assistant coach to alert the leaker when to go and everyone else to listen for the call "Aces," the green light to give a foul. No call, no foul. I also remind them to make a play on the ball when giving the foul.

The other team works the clock for the last shot. We give the first foul at 10 seconds, and I decide not to signal the next foul-to-give. The other team reacts as if it is coming, however, and rushes a shot and misses. We get the rebound and the rebounder finds the leaking guard, and while his pass is short, the guard corrals it well enough, takes two dribbles, and scores, beating the buzzer by a second. We go into the half up by two, with the potential for a four-point swing

and a modest reversal of momentum. The locker room is upbeat, and
team focus has returned. We win by six.

Foul intelligence—a well-designed system for handling foul situations—fuels team success. Effective use of foul situations can determine games. For example, the art of drawing fouls and avoiding careless
fouls can give teams the edge in a game. Conversely, excessive fouling
gifts advantages to the other team, including scoring with a stopped
clock, opportunities to substitute players or change defenses, a means
to protect a lead, registering an old-school three-point play, and compromising substitution rotations, among other problems.

Not all fouls are created equal. Consider that the all-time NBA leader in fouls is Hall of Famer Kareem Abdul-Jabbar. And while Abdul-
Jabbar also recorded the most minutes of any NBA player, and thus
could be expected to pile up fouls, he was a highly intelligent player
who made the NBA All-Defensive Team 11 times. During his prodig-
ious career, he used fouls to his advantage. This underscores that to
enjoy success teams must understand the difference between "good"
fouls, which yield advantage, and "bad" fouls, which lessen team prospects.

GOOD AND BAD FOULS

Coaches should teach their teams what they classify as "good" and "bad"
fouls, and point them out whenever they arise.

Good Fouls (Fouls for Advantage)

- *The Hustle Foul*. Coaches want defense played with urgency. When
  that happens, for example, a player who is whistled for a foul while
  diving on the floor for a loose ball, it is often effort that inspires
  teammates, stokes fans, advances defensive strategy, and pays long-
  term dividends.
- *Fouling While Boxing Out*. Similar to the hustle foul, a well-executed
  (but maybe overzealous) box-out can result in a foul call. Coaches

should nonetheless encourage the effort. Preventing offensive rebounds is crucial.

- *Trying to Take a Charge.* Taking charges is part art, part courage. Sometimes the effort results in a block call, but the more it is practiced and attempted, the higher the incidence of success. The charge call takes away a possession, changes game momentum, and adds to the foul count of the other team.
- *Fouls-to-Give at the End of the Game.* This situation deserves a separate section and is addressed more fully later in this chapter.
- *Fouls to Stop the Clock.* When in catch-up mode late in the game, fouling can be imperative to stop the clock and extend the game, even at the risk of foul shots. The gained advantage is adding time for possessions and hopefully trading no points or one point for two or three points.
- *Fouling a Poor Foul Shooter.* When fouling to stop the clock, isolating a poor free-throw shooter means playing the odds: The advantage gained from clock stoppage (and a shortened possession) is assumed to be greater than the points likely suffered at the foul line.
- *Fouls to Prevent an Easy Score.* It happens all too often—a defender is beat to the basket and ends up committing a "touch" foul that puts the shooter on the line for a possible third point. The alternative is a hard (and clean) play on the ball that prevents the shot and forces the offensive player to earn two (and not three) points.
- *Fouls to Stop a Developing Fast Break.* If your opponent has an open field in transition, unless you face a NBA-type clear-path rule, a defender can foul either to prevent two easy points or, if in the bonus, force the player to earn two points at the line. The gained advantage is minimizing or eliminating a scoring opportunity.
- *Hard Fouls on Dribble Penetration.* A team that protects the basket with hard, legal fouls on the ball sends a message that access to the rim comes with a price, which can inhibit tendencies to attack the basket. The gained advantage is psychological: deterring the other team from entering the paint area.
- *Fouls to Prevent a Three-Point Shot Opportunity in a Three-Point Game.* This subject deserves a separate discussion, which can be found later in this chapter.

Bad Fouls (Fouls That Can Diminish the Likelihood of Team Success)

- *Technicals.* While technicals can motivate players in certain circumstances and even lead to a make-up call, generally they are not good. A technical foul in high school counts as both a personal and a team foul. Worse, if the player manages to draw two technicals in the same game, the player is not only ejected, but also, in some jurisdictions, ineligible to suit up for the next game. Moreover, technicals often occur late in the game, when a team can least afford to lose a possession and gift the other side free throws. Avoiding them, however, is not always easy, as they commonly derive from spontaneous frustration. Nonetheless, programs that repeatedly stress emotional control, as well as respect for officials and good mistake response, and have coaches who monitor emotional buildup in games, can minimize them.
- *Reaching on Defense.* The poster child for lazy defense, reaching is rampant. We must repeatedly remind players not to reach but to build good habits. Effective defense flows from stellar footwork.
- *Hand-checking.* The cousin of the reach, hand-checking is less the product of laziness than uncured bad habits. It occurs both with on-the-ball perimeter defense and in post play (especially with two hands or an extended hand in the back).
- *Frustration Fouls.* These are the product of bad "mistake response," a principle every coach should teach. The more you discuss mistake response with players, the more likely they will be to exercise greater control of how they respond to frustration, error, or disappointment in practice and game situations.
- *Bumping a Dribbler.* This is a cousin to the frustration foul. Defenders sometimes are tempted to body ball handlers who have gained a step or two on them rather than sprint ahead and reestablish legal defensive position. Players need to work hard to avoid succumbing to ego and stay focused on regaining defensive advantage and, where appropriate, rely on defensive help.
- *Fouling When Getting Back Late on Defense.* This foul is a member of the frustration-foul family. Defenders characteristically grab and chop to stop progress rather than rely on help defense. Sometimes

players should accept getting beat off the dribble and know that help defense is the systematic solution.

- *Fatigue Fouls.* Tired players often cheat on defense and get careless. A player too tired to deliver the expected level of defense should generally be off the floor.

- *Fouling a Distance from the Basket.* This occurs when the offense has no advantage or is not in a position to score. While often the product of zeal, which generally is a good thing, it is nonetheless bad judgment.

- *Attempting Blocked Shots on Dribble Penetration.* Too many players dream of being shot blockers and, on dribble penetration, try to fulfill that fantasy. The result is often an awkward effort with arms flailing, followed by the obligatory whistle. It is better to set the feet and "wall off" the other player (i.e., jam the offensive player, chest to chest, and stay mobile with two-hands straight up in the air and feet moving laterally).

- *Swinging Arms Downward When Defending a Shooter.* Defensive players are entitled to their space just like offense players, but they have to understand verticality on defense. Practice note: Bringing referees into practice early in the season can be an effective way to teach this and other techniques.

- *Fouling the Jump Shooter.* Running into the legal space of a perimeter shooter and violating the offensive player's right to verticality or running by them (the "fly-by") is all too fashionable thanks, in large part, to the NBA, where this occurs with alarming regularity. Fouling three-point shooters is on the rise. Perimeter defenders should stay down on shooters with a strong close-out and stutter step, which can discourage the shot or reduce the probability of a make, as well as ready them for an up-fake and the dribble drive.

- *Bending the Elbow of an Arm Bar on Offense.* This foul would be more prevalent if more players habitually used the arm bar to protect the ball (a topic for another day). Regardless, players should know the risk of drawing a foul for bending the arm-bar elbow into contact.

- *Over the Back on a Rebound.* This is a good foul–bad foul grey area, as it often can qualify as a hustle foul (see the hustle foul under "Good Fouls"). For the most part, however, the call is the product of bad judgment. When players are beat to the rebound, they should accept their fate and transition to defense.

- *Bailing Out an Out-of-Control or Off-Balance Offensive Player.* Players sometimes attack the basket out of control and get bailed out by a defender who fouls trying to block the shot or body the offensive player. While it is difficult to get players to play off in this situation, it is nonetheless important to insist that they handle these moments with discipline. More often than not, out-of-control offensive players, if left to their own devices, will miss the shot.
- *Driving into a Crowd of Defenders and Drawing an Offensive Foul.* This is the flip side of the offensive player bail out. Too often, players make up their minds to go the basket and get in the air, descending upon a cadre of help defenders, and committing an offensive foul or other turnover. That is why, among other reasons, the basketball gods created the jump stop.
- *The Moving Screen.* The NBA specializes in this foul, and it is not uncommon at other levels. The precautionary rule is simple: It is the job of the teammate receiving the screen to decide how to use the screen. The job of screeners, once set, is to stay still until their teammates have advanced beyond (or rejected) the screen. If the screen does not work, so be it.
- *Trying to Steal the Ball When Trapping.* Trapping players are often tempted to put their hands on the ball. While understandable, their job is to *mirror* the ball with pressure, blur passing-lane vision, get a deflection on a pass, or force a five-second call or timeout. They should not gamble on the hero moment. Any potential steal belongs to teammates hunting passing lanes.
- *Swinging Elbows.* Players facing severe pressure with the ball sometimes swing elbows, only to earn a foul, sometimes flagrant. This lapse of judgment is fixable with drills that stress chinning the ball and using ducking movements when under pressure.

Once players are clear on what you deem good or bad fouls, give them a list with descriptions and consider testing them on the differences to improve their understanding and create the proper mind-set. Make it fun, like a *Family Feud* format, to increase interest and enhance learning. A keen understanding of your philosophy will raise their hoops IQ and improve the quality of individual and team performance.

FOUL-TROUBLE SITUATIONS

Because foul-trouble situations implicate judgment, game instincts, and philosophy, coaches differ on how to handle them. The important point is having a well-considered approach. First, coaching philosophy influences how coaches determine what constitutes foul trouble. Some coaches favor a formula, like when the number of fouls matches the number of the quarter. Thus, a player who gets a second foul in the second quarter (or first half), a third foul in (or before) the third quarter (or early second half), and a fourth foul in (or before) the fourth quarter (or last several minutes of the second half) is in foul trouble. Others are inclined to play each game by ear and make game-specific strategic decisions, depending on game flow, how referees are calling the game, how players are reacting to game intensity, lead differentials, the quality of the bench rotation, and the implications for specific players.

Second, coaches also differ on how to handle key players in foul trouble. Some keep a star player in the game regardless, believing the team can ill afford to have that player sitting. Others bring him to the pine until they perceive it safe or necessary to reinsert him. Jeff Van Gundy offers this interesting insight: "I think coaches sometimes foul their own players out of games by benching them too long when in foul trouble." Still, there is no shame in protecting your impact players, even if that means calling a timeout. This is another know-your-personnel moment that implicates how much you trust players to avoid another foul.

Third, if you want to remove the player in foul trouble, do you always wait for a dead-ball moment? When is it justified to burn a timeout to pull a player in foul trouble? How many times have you second-guessed your decision to wait for the dead-ball whistle, only to see your player get the foul you wanted to avoid? This is also addressed in chapter 1.

Fourth, the flip side is when to reinsert a player in foul trouble into the game. Some coaches prefer to return them to play relatively soon. Some will hold them out to increase the chances they can finish the game if it is a close contest. There is also the concern the player will not play effective defense. A player who has shown a tendency to commit careless fouls probably should not be on the floor. While players in foul trouble must do their part to avoid more fouls, this does mean guarding ineffectively. It means playing smarter and getting more focused on sound defensive fundamentals.

Fifth, while most of us would love to leave our players on autopilot, we need to be realistic about players who need coaching help to succeed. When a coach feels compelled to keep a player in a game despite existing or looming foul trouble, other than telling them "don't pick up another foul," consider adjustments. In man defense, you can change defensive assignments to minimize the risk that the player will pick up another foul. You can employ the offense-to-defense strategy, keeping the vulnerable player on the floor for defense as little as practical. And, of course, you can shift to a zone defense.

DRAWING FOULS

Game-specific situations command seeking contact and a foul call. For example, assume an important opposing player ends up in foul trouble and is kept in the game. Some coaches are reluctant to focus on trying to lure the player into another foul, concerned with undermining game rhythm or plan. While understandable, the converse can force the player out of the game for an extended period of time with various benefits. Consider attacking the player off the dribble or with up-fakes, or isolate the player in pick-and-roll situations to create a mismatch. They may also play soft defense to avoid another foul. Going straight at them on offense might yield an advantage.

Another advantageous draw-the-foul situation occurs when the other team is in the bonus relatively early in the first and second halves. Using aggressive dribble penetration to force contact both on the drive and from help defenders can increase trips to the foul line. This can be a treasure trove of opportunity, monitored by an ever-attentive assistant coach.

FOULS-TO-GIVE SITUATIONS

Games almost always present situations where we direct players to give a foul for various reasons. It is the proverbial "unintentional" intentional foul. How often, however, do we devote practice time to teaching how to effectively give a foul and when to do so?

First, have a code name for when to give the foul. "Give one" and "foul" are not code and highlight the intentional nature of the act. Consider a name or hand signal that at least gives the appearance of keeping things in code and less conspicuous. Referees tend to allow leeway here, but you can't count on it every time. Moreover, it doesn't hurt to let referees know in advance what you have in mind. Regardless, players should make a play on the ball, the best insurance against an intentional foul call and a chance for a steal or held ball.

Second, consider the timing of fouls-to-give when you are ahead. The goal is presumably to disrupt a possession and force a restart of the offense with less time on the clock until there are no more fouls to give. As such, your team needs to know when and, conversely, when not to commit the foul. Do you wait until the dribbler puts the ball on the floor, for a specified number of dribbles or for a pass or two? The foul can be effective when the dribbler first moves north–south toward the basket. It holds less value if the ball is at or near halfcourt, the other team has not initiated a play, or the dribbler is moving east to west. Ideally, you want the other team to use some clock, which means the timing can be tricky, especially if you have not practiced this situation.

Third, fouling presents different considerations when you are behind in the game. The overriding goal is to extend the game and increase possessions. The two main factors are time on the clock and the lead differential. In an ideal world, we want turnovers and quick stops. But this can be wishful thinking. At some point, you have to trade the ability of the other team to make foul shots against the ability of your team to have profitable possessions at the other end in as little time as practicable.

There is no bright line here. One approach is to foul after the first or second pass if a turnover has not occurred. Or, if the other team is rebounding, you can try to steal the inbound pass, and failing that, foul the inbound receiver. Another is having your team play aggressively for a possession or two to cause a turnover since fouling is acceptable in the situation. In addition, consider fouling during the dead-ball moments (i.e., before the ball is entered, provided the rules do not impose undesirable consequences in that situation).

Another approach is a formula. This is covered more expansively in chapter 7 (End-of-Game Situations), but by way of example, if in a three-possession game, consider fouling when the three-minute mark approaches. In that situation, you can conservatively assume four possessions (and hopefully more) for each team. Because you cannot assume three stops and three scores in of four possessions, you may want to start fouling after the clock dips below the three-minute mark. You can delay execution of the strategy for one possession after the three-minute mark, but waiting longer is risky.

Fourth, who should commit the fouls? A designated fouler allows others to stay out of foul trouble and can give another player a blow. Or if that is not practical or desirable, next in line is a player on the floor with fewer fouls.

Fifth, knowing which player to foul is not always easy. As discussed in chapter 7, before each game, have a list of players to foul that you can review with the team pregame and during an applicable timeout. If you cannot isolate a weak foul shooter with the ball, try to trap or double-team a ball handler using the defender guarding a weak foul shooter to force the "habit" pass out of the double-team to the now-open player so they can be fouled. That said, while you do not want a good foul shooter on the line, it might be difficult to isolate a weak-shooting player with the ball, forcing you, if stopping the clock is paramount, to foul anyone with the ball and take your chances.

Sixth, players must be reminded to play the whistle. Especially late in games, referees do not always give you the foul call on your cue. Everyone must be alert to deploy the strategy until the whistle blows.

Finally, consider using the foul-to-give strategy at the end of first half if you believe you can foil a possession or two as time winds down. This is explored more in chapter 4.

WHETHER TO FOUL TO AVOID THE THREE-POINT SHOT

Should you foul when up three points in the last several seconds of a game to eliminate the possibility of a three-point shot? Many coaches defend for the stop. This is consistent with how they played the game until the three-up situation arose; furthermore, coaches often believe fouling conveys a lack of confidence in team defense. The risk is ending up in overtime on the make or, worse, losing if the shooter cans the three and is fouled in the act.

This is about probabilities. Are you more likely to win in regulation if you don't foul and risk allowing a three-point shot or if you foul and chance what follows from the foul shots? While reasonable minds might differ, I believe the probabilities favor fouling in the last several seconds.

Absent a turnover, the other team will likely get a shot off. Even assuming a tough shot, because of time pressure, there is probably at least a one in four (or better) chance that they will make the three and send the game into overtime. Contrast this with the opposite worst-case scenario: you foul intentionally and the other team makes the first foul shot, purposely misses the second shot, gets the offensive rebound, and puts the ball up to tie the game or, even more unlikely, finds a shooter on the perimeter for a three to win the game, all in a matter of several seconds. The odds of this happening are low and much less likely to happen than the other scenario, especially if your team is prepared.

AVOIDING GAME-ENDING THREE-POINT SHOTS

If you intend to foul, the issue becomes how to execute the plan. You must consider the following:

- How much time do you want on the clock when you commit the foul?
- Who do you foul? Do you foul the dribbler or a pass receiver?
- Where on the floor do you foul? Ten feet from three-point arc? When the dribbler crosses halfcourt? On the first pass after crossing halfcourt? On the catch of the anticipated catch-and-shoot?

Consider these approaches: 1) If the other team starts the possession at three-quarters or full court, foul the dribbler crossing the halfcourt line; 2) if the possession begins on the sideline or under the basket, or you can't get to the ball handler at midcourt, foul the first pass receiver on the catch. Bear in mind, especially after a timeout, that the other side might prepare for the foul and try a quick catch-and-shoot. This is why it is crucial to foul on the catch or as the catch is in progress, as is thoughtful screen defense.

You should also practice this situation from the perspective of being down three points, specifically these scenarios: 1) a relatively quick three on a catch-and-shoot; 2) a quick foul, followed by a plan that contemplates missing the second free throw (see the next section); 3) a press that seeks to force a turnover on the inbounds play or shortly after the ball is entered; and 4) preparing for full-court pressure to minimize time used coming up the court.

WHEN TO PURPOSEFULLY MISS A FOUL SHOT

While rare, as recounted in the preface, situations do arise when you have to consider missing a foul shot on purpose. Here are three end-of-the-game situations where it can happen.

First, your team is down two or three points, has one foul shot left, and doesn't have enough time for another good offensive possession, for example, six seconds or less left on the clock. If you make the foul shot, you end up on defense still down one or two points with precious little time on the clock. You have to foul immediately after the inbounds pass to stop the clock and put the other team on the line. Then, after the foul shots are taken, you are either in a two-possession game, in which case you are effectively done, or you have to travel the full length of the court and make a shot in a few seconds. Alternatively, you can go for the steal on the inbounds pass. If that fails, however, you will suffer precious clicks off the clock, especially if you overplay. The probability of success in this scenario, started by a made foul shot, is quite low. The odds of success are improved if you miss the shot, hoping to get the offensive rebound and another scoring opportunity.

Second, you are nursing a one-point lead and are on the line with one free throw left, with only a few seconds on the clock. Canning the shot, giving you a two-point lead, makes it more difficult to lose in regulation. It also allows you to set up your defense comfortably. On the other hand, a make allows the other team to call a timeout and set up a play and look for an opportunity to make something happen.

A purposeful miss in this situation, however, has various benefits. It takes one or two precious seconds off the clock, and if you rebound the miss, the window is shut on the other team. Thus, you first need to decide whether to put players on the line to rebound or keep them back in a defensive posture. If the miss is executed well and you stack the lane lines, you might get the rebound, hold the ball, and ice the game. If the other team gets the rebound, while miracles do happen, it is highly improbable they will either toss the ball more than 80 feet for a make or move the ball to a spot on the floor where they can get a decent look for a long three-point attempt. The odds of either happening are even lower if you contest the full-length shot or contain the ball handler to slow the movement up the floor.

Third, your team is ahead and on the line, and the remaining foul shot will result in a three-point lead with a few or slightly more seconds left in the game. Do you miss this shot or try for the three-point lead and a dead-ball moment that allows the other team to set up something? This is a tougher call. On balance, to increase the probability of a win, the odds favor making the shot and getting the three-point lead. If you deliberately miss, there is a chance the other team will rebound and get off a long-distance three, while your defense is unsettled. While that is improbable, you can lower the odds even more with a make. If you make the foul shot you are now up three; can set up your defense (possibly with a timeout or substitution); and, if necessary to avoid the three-point attempt, can foul the other team on the inbounds pass, giving them two shots with the clock almost wound down and the game virtually over.

HOW TO PURPOSEFULLY MISS A FOUL SHOT

Once committed to missing a foul shot, the question is *how* to miss? For example, if looking to end the game on the miss, consider missing glass to rim—top right for a right-handed shooter and top left for a left-handed shooter. This sets up a likely high rebound and a scramble that will use clock. Shoot the ball softly for ball control. A hard shot might result in failure to hit the rim, a violation that stops the clock and gives the other team possession.

If you need to get the possession and score, however, as in the scenario in the preface, the player on the line should shoot the ball hard off the front-middle of the rim as soon as the referee delivers the ball—

before the other team gets set in the lane. While this is no easy task, if practiced enough, the ball will come straight back to the shooter. If you get the rebound, you have three options: shoot immediately if you need two points, outlet to a three-pointer shooter, or, if practical, and necessary, call timeout.

Finally, practice these situations from the opposite perspective as well.

- You are up by two points, and the other team has one foul shot remaining with time only for an offensive rebound and quick putback. Prepare your players for the quick, purposeful miss with sound boxing-out fundamentals.
- You are up three or less, and the other team has one foul shot and time for a rebound and kick out for a three. Be alert for the purposeful miss, and identify and cover the three-point shooters. Remind players to defend with hands up to avoid a foul and reduce the make percentage.
- You are down by one, with a few seconds left, and the other team has one free throw left and likely will miss purposefully. Be ready to rebound and throw the ball the length of the court on the catch.

✿ ✿ ✿

Strategies for addressing foul situations have both static and dynamic elements. It is important to have a system and set of rules when they apply and when the probabilities call for a departure from structure. The interplay among the coaching staff is particularly important so that everyone is on the same page and players understand what is expected of them.

3

SUBSTITUTIONS

"I never substitute just to substitute. I play my regulars. The only way a guy gets off the floor is if he dies."—Abe Lemons

We are in a physically challenging game and whistles are blowing almost as often as basketball shoes are squeaking. The odds of losing players to foul disqualification are high. In anticipation, I play virtually the entire team in the first half to keep everyone fresh in case we must rely on a deep rotation more so than usual. This is risky because in this game we can ill afford too many bad possessions. Regardless, I want to avoid asking cold bench players to bail us out.

True enough, we approach crunch time with our starting backcourt on the bench, disqualified by fouls. And to make matters worse, we are down 10. I gaze down the bench to the stark reality that substitution options are less than ideal. In addition to our backup point guard, I choose a talented but streaky shooter who has managed to evade the art of playing defense most of his playing days. If, however, his hot hand from the first half continues—he canned two threes—we might pull off a comeback.

Upon entering the contest, he drains three straight threes and puts us back in the game. I move to an offense-to-defense substitution strategy. I keep the hot shooter in the game as much as possible and substitute for him with a stalwart defensive player (also off the bench) who does a great job helping us get stops. We capture the momentum; get dialed in; and, after some nerve-racking back and forth near the end, manage to win by three.

Coaches typically undergo trial and error to evolve to a substitution philosophy and style that suits them. Furthermore, because philosophy and style can differ and change throughout time, coaches are wise to reevaluate their substitution approach from time to time. But whichever approach a coach employs, substitution decisions are most effective when they focus on both short-term and long-term success. While not intended as an exhaustive list, here are some questions to ponder.

- *Core Philosophy*: Do you have an equality-based (egalitarian) approach that seeks to distribute playing opportunities relatively evenly? Do you, in contrast, use a strict meritocracy system that challenges players to earn playing opportunities? Or does your philosophy fall somewhere in between?
- *Long-Term Focus*: Do you share minutes liberally earlier in the season and take greater risks early in the season to build confidence and trust, and create greater depth for down the road to address fatigue, injury, illness, and foul trouble?
- *Short-Term Focus*: Do you like to play most or all of your bench players early in games to increase their readiness for second-half situations?
- *Personal Inclinations*: Do you have a natural reluctance to trust certain players to perform? In other words, are you stingy with game opportunities?
- *Habits*: Do you have specific substitution routines, for example, using a certain player at the same time of a period or half?
- *Practice Style*: To what extent are these various considerations reflected in how you run practices—that is, do you mix the composition of your 5-on-5 groups or typically keep the starting five and first rotation on one team and the balance of your squad on the other?

You might also ask yourself the following: Is your *expressed* philosophy consistent with your *actual* substitution decisions? A gap can exist between what seems philosophically sound and what is actually done in game situations. The more introspective and honest we are in assessing whether our presumed values line up with the substitutions decisions we actually make, the more effective our decision making.

ALLOCATION OF RESPONSIBILITY

Many head coaches prefer to handle game substitutions. Others delegate the responsibility to assistants to free themselves up to concentrate on other game matters. In either case, it is important to discuss anticipated substitution decisions in advance of each game to ground game strategy and minimize confusion, stress, and potential disagreement in the heat of battle. You can always depart from a plan, but having a method of attack provides a useful point of reference.

An assigned assistant should track the other bench for impending substitutions, especially during timeouts. While this can be difficult in the flow of a game, detecting the substitution decisions of the other team before their new player gets on the floor can allow for an effective counter.

Players should be keyed to substitution thinking, especially substitution patterns and their particular roles, for example, whom they normally replace and when. Players who know when they routinely enter games for a particular teammate can study defensive assignments and focus on what else is expected of them defensively and offensively. While there should be no confusion about matchups, it happens. How many times have you heard a substitute ask the player being replaced, "Who are you guarding?" or worse, "What defense are we in?"

Related, constant communication with players about their role, especially as it changes during the season, will increase player morale and capacity (and willingness) to perform. When we change the role of a player, especially for an upcoming game, the player should know sufficiently in advance so they can adjust mentally to the change. Consider laying a foundation for substitution roles and patterns before the season, whether in summer league or in whatever other context the team plays as a group. Realistic expectations are important to ensure game readiness.

SUBSTITUTION RULES AND BEHAVIORAL EXPECTATIONS

Coaches should review the substitution rules and procedures with players at the start of the season—with occasional reminders. While many of the following suggestions may be self-evident, reminders are prudent. It is never endearing to have referees remind players and coaches to do what should be second nature and well understood. It reflects poorly on players and coaching staff alike. They might seem like minor things, but the more your players handle themselves well, the more credibility they will enjoy with officials. Here is a checklist:

- Players should enter the game with their jerseys tucked in.
- Substitutes should move to the designated spot in front of the scorer's table.
- Substitutes should report specifically to the official scorer.
- Substitutes should wait until the referee waves them in before coming onto the floor.
- Replaced players should run off the floor and interact with the substitute about the defensive assignment and vice versa.
- The entire bench should greet players coming off the floor.
- When a substitution during foul shots is designed to stop the action, the substitution should not report to the scorer's table until after the referee delivers the ball to the foul shooter on the final foul shot; reporting beforehand will bring the sub into the game before the foul shot and foil the stoppage strategy. In contrast, a substitution for a player in foul trouble should seek entry into the game on the first foul shot to avoid keeping the substituted player in the game if the last foul shot is missed.

SPECIFIC SITUATIONS

Coaches often are challenged to make substitution adjustments in the blink of an eye. Fundamental to effective substituting is a keen knowledge of players' skill strengths and weaknesses, and performance tendencies. And while the methods for using substitutions are generally no secret, the value of reminders cannot be understated.

1. *Defensive Adjustments*. Defensive adjustment substitutions may be the most creative of all, and they run the gamut, for example, inserting a defensive specialist to control an opposing player who is lighting it up offensively, countering an opposing substitution that has created an

unfavorable matchup, putting in the group that plays a specific defense the best (e.g., a match-up zone), injecting high-energy defenders to offset sluggishness, and inserting rebounders to decrease the opposition's second-chance opportunities.

2. *Offensive Adjustments*. In instances where you are behind late in a game, you might have to insert more perimeter shooters, which might mean poorer defenders and diluted rebounding. You might need to insert better ball handlers to confront a press or ball pressure. You might also substitute to rebalance the offense because of a defensive substitution that sacrifices offensive firepower. And, as noted in the prior chapter, when ahead late in the game, consider having your best foul shooters on the floor to offset the opposing team's strategy to give fouls.

3. *Matchup Substitutions*. Substitutions to change defensive and offensive matchups are an integral part of the chess-playing dimension of coaching, and when they work, coaches can justifiably claim a gold star. These can be straightforward, like trying to force a rim protector away from the basket with a big who can shoot the midrange or perimeter shot, or forcing a smaller player to guard an effective post-up player and create a "mouse in the house" moment. Others are not so easy and depend on more subtle factors, for example, forcing a matchup between a player with strong dribble-drive skills and a defender who habitually reaches on penetration, especially when your team is in the bonus. The essential ingredients are tracking tendencies and patterns in games and the ever-important know your personnel (KYP).

4. *Poor Play*. A frequent sore spot in the coach–player relationship arises when coaches remove (or appear to remove) players in response to game errors. Sitting can be a great motivator, and some coaches do not hesitate to yank players for committing certain mistakes. That said, with every generational change, player skin seems to get a little thinner. A general environment where a single error will condemn a player to the bench can be counterproductive, create an atmosphere of great stress, and induce tentative play.

Again, how well do you know your players? Certain players will react positively to coming off the floor, using it as an opportunity to reboot and get ready for the next time they enter the game. Others get frustrated, especially if they have just begun to find game rhythm. What about a quick refresher? Players can be nervous coming off the bench, especially for the first time in a game, and may only need a quick spell to settle down, refocus, and receive a few encouraging words before being reinserted. How should you handle their respective responses? And, importantly, do you have an established routine to address the performance issues that bring players to the bench? Who handles the communication, you or an assistant? A more difficult question is how long to allow a player to play through mistakes. How good is their "mistake response"?

5. *The One-Dimensional or Limited Player.* Most teams have at least one player who defends well but is limited offensively or vice versa. Finding ways to obtain sufficient contributions from this player, while minimizing risks associated with the weaknesses, can be difficult. One solution, of course, is to keep the player on the bench. But games present situations when you need more defense than offense and the reverse. The solution often is found in partnering the player with certain teammates to maximize strengths on one end of the floor, while minimizing weaknesses on the other.

6. *Offense-to-Defense.* This is a more refined version of the preceding substitution and may be the most strategically delicate of any substitution decision. Ideally, we can create late-game advantages with the best offensive combination on the floor when we have the ball and the best defensive combination on the floor at the other end. The problem, of course, is that many times they are not the same five players. This type of substitution requires attention to game flow and keen anticipation of dead ball-situations, and what to do if the dead-ball whistle does not happen at the moment your strategic script desires. At the end of the day, each offense-to-defense substitution must line up with a strategic purpose.

7. *The Single-Possession Substitution.* This is similar to offense-for-defense substitution and typically occurs at the end of a quarter when a coach at the defensive end does not want to risk a player getting a foul and replaces them only for the last possession.

8. *Disruption of Flow.* A well-timed substitution can momentarily disrupt game pace or flow. Using the dead-ball situation, you can slow down transition, stop momentum, or set up full-court pressure or another defensive system that requires a few extra seconds to get ready.

9. *Managing Player Confidence.* While not all coaches agree on how to handle it, a substitution can enhance player confidence. For example,

you might be tempted, depending on your risk adversity, to leave a player who normally gets limited floor opportunities in the game to increase overall comfort on the floor, especially if the player has performed effectively. From a different perspective, does substituting a player who has consistently performed well build or undermine confidence? Most players who play well believe they have earned the right to stay on the floor. Others, however, might feel more positive about themselves, perhaps not right away but ultimately, if taken off the floor after an effective run or on a positive note (and before their performance slips), especially when unaccustomed to extended minutes. This is another judgment call that implicates how well you know (and manage) your personnel.

10. *Spreading Out Minutes in Decided Games*. When games are (or seem) well in hand—sometimes a grey area—when do you empty the bench to provide playing opportunities and build playing comfort for players deep in the rotation? When to substitute on the lead continuum depends on style, philosophy, and your personal jitter quotient. There is also the question of how to substitute in this situation, specifically whether to keep the new group on the floor balanced or mix things up. Do you phase better players out or make wholesale changes? Phasing out enhances stability and allows new players the benefit of working with more talented ones, which reduces stress, establishes comfort levels, and builds confidence. Wholesale substitutions, on the other hand, provide more minutes to the last rotation.

11. *Creativity*. Unforeseeable developments can wreak havoc on the best laid coaching plans. Injuries, illnesses, and suspensions can compel us to toss philosophy and routine to the winds in favor of something we otherwise would be unlikely to consider, like asking a player to embrace an unfamiliar role.

Basketball aficionados will recall one of the most celebrated examples of this thinking in Game 5 of the 1980 NBA Finals between the Los Angeles Lakers and Philadelphia 76ers, when Lakers center Kareem Abdul-Jabbar suffered a serious ankle injury, relegating him to watching Game 6 from home. Lakers coach Paul Westhead inserted rookie point guard Magic Johnson at center (and later at guard and forward). Johnson delivered one of the most storied performances in NBA Finals history—42 points, 15 rebounds, and 7 assists—as the Lakers won Game 6 and captured the NBA title. Radical situations sometimes call for radical solutions outside the four corners of the playbook.

12. *The Nonsubstitution.* Coaches are creatures of habit. We are often compelled to rely on our best players or starters at certain points of a game. There are, however, situations where nonstarters can get the job done, and toying with an effective combination is shortsighted. Consider the maxim, "If it ain't broke, don't fix it."

NBA enthusiasts may recall the decision of Kevin McHale of the Houston Rockets to stay with a winning floor combination against the Los Angeles Clippers in the sixth game of the second round of the 2015 Western Conference playoffs—a closeout game for the Clippers. McHale kept his star and the league's leading scorer, James Harden, on the bench for the entire fourth quarter as Rockets subs delivered one of the most improbable comebacks in NBA playoff history, outscoring the Clippers, 40–15, in the final frame to take game 6 (and then winning game 7 to advance the Western Conference Finals).

13. *Enforcement of Team Rules and Discipline.* Every now and then—hopefully not too often—we substitute for a player who has acted improperly. Whether to remove a player when this happens depends on a confluence of style, rule enforcement, consistency, the perceived need for discipline, and knowledge of the player. Some behavior cannot be tolerated and compels a substitution, for example, overt disrespect for referees or coaches, or threatening or out of control behavior. Sportsmanship and respect matter.

14. *Fresh Players.* Have you ever kept key players in so long they slow down when their contributions are needed most? Asking key players to play for, for example, 90 percent or more of a game can backfire. There are many ways to provide them with ample rest without keeping them off the floor too long. For instance, you can substitute them out for one minute here and there or give them longer breaks with a substitution at the end of the quarter so they get the benefit of both bench time and the quarter break. However you prefer to handle this scenario, be mindful of having five fresh players on the floor at all times. Tired players easily become prone to making mistakes, especially on defense.

15. *Fatigue.* On a related topic, most players will not own up to the need for a break, even though the signs are conspicuous to the coaching staff, for example, shots falling short, tugging at shorts, slower move-

ment down the floor, and lazy defense. Sometimes coaches have to initiate the substitution.

Consider a specific signal to ask for a break. Two common calls are the jersey tug and the fist. A signal gets the job done at the earliest time and underscores the importance of recognizing the fatigue moment. Moreover, laud players who have the team orientation to ask for a rest, as this positive reinforcement can be infectious. You can also reward them by reinserting them into the game as soon as they announce they are ready.

16. *Injury*. While injury substitutions are commonplace, the situation becomes complex if the injured player must exit with foul shots to take. Do you substitute your best foul shooter on the bench even if they are not the ideal substitution and risk not being able to remove them soon enough? Or do you choose the best substitute regardless? If late in a close game, you might opt for the best foul shooter. Otherwise, it might not matter.

17. *Substitutions Related to Fouls*. This subject, with its many subparts, including fouls to give, strategic fouling, and enhancing foul shot capability, is covered in the preceding chapter.

18. *The Messenger Substitution*. This is discussed in chapter 1 as one of the "free" timeouts.

19. *Platoons*. Some coaches, notably John Calipari at Kentucky, Roy Williams at North Carolina, and Coach K at Duke, occasionally employ a two-platoon (or "posse") system that consists of two five-player groups instead of the single-player substitution system. Similarly, the "Grinnell System," an uptempo style that coach Dave Arseneault developed at Grinnell College, modeled on the run-and-gun system of coach Paul Westhead, features frequent platoon substitutions. A platoon system can keep players fresh (which is especially useful for transition or pressing teams), distribute opportunities, boost morale and confidence, keep players out of foul trouble, and cause matchup challenges for opposing coaches.

On the other hand, many of these benefits are available with select substitutions, which in turn allow greater flexibility. An effective platoon system also depends on personnel depth, which the aforementioned coaches often enjoy. Another downside is that platoon players might become most comfortable and familiar with only the teammates in their platoon group, which could impact floor chemistry, especially if

injury or illness intervene. Also, platoon substitutions, if applied system-
atically, can undermine game rhythm. Why, for example, change a platoon group when a player has a hot hand or the unit is playing great
team defense, or, conversely, stay with an ineffective group longer than
scripted.

A variation on the platoon system is to substitute in smaller num-
bers, like two or three at a time, until five new players are on the floor.
This allows the first substitution rotation to find their game rhythm
while playing with starters. It also takes pressure off the substitutions to
step up immediately. The next group can draw from the stability of this
initial substitution rotation. Another variation is to use the platoon con-
cept only in the first half to rest the starting five for one or two minutes.
This allows starters to rest as a group and return with greater energy. It
also might present matchup problems for the other side.

On balance, a platoon substitution system seems a good idea in rare
situations—when a coach has significant talent depth—and, even then,
it should be employed more strategically than automatically to allow for
maximum effectiveness in game situations.

20. *The Finishing Team.* A cousin to the platoon system is a team
with the best five game finishers on the floor, whether starters or not,
like the Golden State Warrior "Death Lineup." Many factors, for example, foul trouble, foul shooting (when ahead), offensive power (when
behind), ball-handling skills (end of the game), and matchups, will dic-
tate who should be on the floor during crunch time. Consideration
should also be given to which players habitually rise to the occasion
when game pressure is greatest. Certain players are nails under pressure. Crunch time presents the quintessential KYP moment and triggers how much a coach trusts certain players to close out games. Said
John Wooden, "It's not so important who starts the game but who
finishes it."

✿ ✿ ✿

Deploying players in game situations is as much a chess game as anything coaches do to win games. It is where knowledge of personnel—
ours and theirs—is tested the most, and we are called upon to realistically assess the ability of our players to perform in specific situations. A
well-considered substitution system, honed in practice through combi-

nations and situations, will increase consistency and effectiveness of game performance.

4

END-OF-QUARTER SITUATIONS

"We have a great bunch of outside shooters. Unfortunately, all our games are played indoors."—Weldon Drew

We are in command of a preseason, nonleague game as halftime approaches. Since late in the first quarter, we have enjoyed a consistent two-digit lead and withstood the other team's runs. Because I want us to better appreciate that every possessions counts, no matter what the situation, I call a timeout to review our final possession of the half with 16 seconds remaining before the break. The lesson is well worth burning the timeout.

Our point guard is smart and knows the folly of forcing action and the value of finding high-percentage opportunities. We decide to go with a 1–4 set that has several options. I tell the point guard to attack the paint at 10 seconds looking for options and expect a convergence of help defense on penetration. I instruct everyone that in the instance of a make, they should match up immediately and defend full court with enough separation to eliminate foul risk and force the other team to consume the precious remaining seconds coming up the floor.

True to form, our guy at the point breaks his man down, and as he penetrates, our wings crisscross and curl back up to the three-point area. As expected, he draws a barrage of help defense, and before he engages the scurrying defenders, he jump stops in the lane, up-fakes to freeze the defense, pivots, and kicks to an open shooter on the right wing, who drains a three, putting us up by 17. We match up well on the make, and the half ends.

In the locker room, while I commend the team for a great half of basketball, I spend most of the time regaling the vital importance of every possession of every game and how that mindset, which they displayed with great skill just moments ago, will elevate them to a higher level.

The end of the first three quarters in high school basketball and the first half at the college level present common situations for opportunity: 1) the 2-for-1, 2) taking the last shot with the shot clock off, 3) defending the last possession with the shot clock off, and 4) giving fouls at the end of the first half. A fifth and similar situation is how to handle a dwindling shot clock on defense. Each situation is sufficiently discrete to deserve specific game plans. The end of the fourth quarter or end-of-game situations, including overtime, are more complex and implicate the use of different strategic considerations and are addressed separately in chapters 5 and 12.

SITUATION: THE 2-FOR-1

In shot clock jurisdictions, 2-for-1 situations—when your team has the first of three theoretically remaining possessions—occur in virtually every game. The goal is not merely to take an early shot to preserve the last shot of the quarter, as any team can quickly throw something at the rim. A quick, low-percentage shot will likely mean a wasted possession, a euphemism for turnover. The goal is a good shot as soon as circumstances permit.

The first question is how much time should remain before implementing the 2-for-1 set? A 35-second shot clock means the 2-for-1 situation occurs when you have the ball with less than 70 and more than 35 seconds left in the quarter (or in college, obtaining possessions with between 60 and 30 seconds left in the first half). Obviously, if the clock shows, for example, 37 seconds (or 32 seconds in college) and you have to move the ball the entire length of the court, it is not an ideal 2-for-1 moment. If inclined to try to tease two possessions out of the end of a period, you should first decide what is a relatively comfortable range of time on the clock to trigger the 2-for-1 call and also know when in that range you prefer to take the first shot of the first possession. While coaches differ, a relatively safe approach in high school is taking the first shot between 46 and 50 seconds. This allows a chance for an offensive putback and—assuming the other team uses most of the shot clock in the next possession—leaves approximately 10 or more seconds for a second possession. You can adjust accordingly in college to reflect the five-second difference in shot clocks.

Of course, if the clock does not allow the luxury of the ideal situation, you might decide not to implement the strategy. For example, if you have the ball at the halfcourt with closer to 40 seconds left in the quarter, you may be better off winding down the clock before taking a shot to limit the time your opponent has for the last shot of the quarter. If you have an effective (oft-practiced) quick hitter, you have more flexibility. But be realistic and seconds-conscious to avoid a bad possession and counterproductive result. To control risk, you might limit use of the 2-for-1 strategy to the first half, when there is less urgency than in the second half, when there might be a premium on getting an excellent shot.

Finally, how do you alert the troops to execute a 2-for-1? Many coaches actually call "2-for-1" or "two-fer," or flash two fingers to signal the strategy. This works, but consider a specific code that is not obvious to the other side to minimize anticipated defensive adjustments.

SITUATION: SHOT CLOCK OFF AND TAKING THE LAST SHOT

The goal here is self-evident: a high-percentage shot that leaves insufficient time for a meaningful (or any) possession at the other end. The benefits are substantial. A score and no possession for the opponent could mean a swing of four to six points and a lift going into the upcoming break. Here are several considerations.

First, does your team have a rule for what shots may be taken at certain clock points at the end of a quarter; for instance, an uncontested layup at any time during the possession, the best shot possible at eight seconds or less, or no shot if you cannot get any good looks other than a buzzer beater (to prevent other team from getting a possession)? Players need imposed discipline here.

Second, when do you initiate the play in the last possession of the quarter: 12, 10, or 8 seconds or some other time? Many teams let the clock tick below 10 seconds, which can push the envelope. Good defense or poor execution can foil this plan and bring a bad shot. You also may want to leave some clock—two or three seconds, for example—for a second-chance opportunity. In last-shot situations, defenses tend to overhelp, which increases offensive rebounding chances.

Consider designing something to keep the defense moving. Too many teams isolate in this situation and often end up with a poor shot. You may add a small cushion to allow recovery from a mistake or unanticipated complication. Thus, you might initiate a quick hitter with six to eight seconds left and a more complicated play with 10 to 12 seconds left to play. Do what fits your personnel.

Third, on a related point, when do want your team to take the shot at the end of the quarter? At less than eight seconds? Less than five? Again, think about inserting a time cushion for a second-chance opportunity.

Many teams in this situation shoot too early, take a bad shot, and allow the other team to close the period with ample time for a good possession. Again, a bad early shot is functionally a turnover. This is especially important if the possession arrow is pointing your way, giving you the first possession in the next period. Rather than take a bad shot and give up a possession, your team may be better off with a buzzer shot. On the other hand, waiting too long can present a problem as well, resulting in a rushed shot and a naked possession. There is admittedly a fine line between shooting too early and too late. But it is a line coaches should constantly strive to draw with vigilant practice work.

Fourth, what do you run? In this situation, you may want a play you normally do not use during the game. Too many teams call familiar plays in this situation. Most teams are well scouted. Calling a known game play for this situation reduces the chances for success.

Fifth, is the bench trained to count down the last 10 seconds? Too often this important contribution is practiced inconsistently. It should be routine.

Sixth, if you get a quick score, what defense do you set up? Do you greet them at halfcourt and play straight up? Do you instead apply full-court pressure to force them out of their comfort zone? And as discussed in the prior chapter, do you use a substitution on the make to allow your team to set up defensively? Whatever your druthers, consider practicing this situation as a combined offensive and defensive plan.

Finally, if you get the last possession at the opposite end with 10 seconds or less on the clock, you likely lack breathing room to run a halfcourt set or even a quick hitter and thus need a separate strategy and play. Do you allow your inbound receiver to dribble furiously down the floor and make a decision on the fly before the defense can get organized? Do you run something specific that includes screens and long passes? Regardless of what you prefer, it is useful to have a precise play for this situation for both ends of periods and the end of a game. (See the discussion in chapter 8 about the famous Danny Ainge full-court play.)

SITUATION: SHOT CLOCK OFF AND DEFENDING

Needless to say, at minimum here we want a stop on a high note entering the next session. The first consideration is whether to spring a surprise on the other team to confuse them and perhaps generate a turnover. For example, after a make (whether via a field goal or foul shot), consider pressing full court or at least applying full-court ball pressure to cause the other team to use clock. Also consider changing defenses, like throwing a zone at them to generate confusion and force the other team to work harder and use clock. In addition, consider halfcourt traps or fouls-to-give (see the next section and chapter 1). And, of course, you can always rely on straight-up man-to-man defense.

SITUATION: FOULS-TO-GIVE AT THE END OF THE FIRST HALF

Although fouls-to-give are covered in chapter 2, they bear brief mention here, as not all coaches think to give fouls in the first half in a favorable foul situation. Giving fouls before the bonus is triggered can foil a last possession in the first half, as well as the end of a game. If you subscribe to the principle that every possession holds importance, taking one away before the teams break for halftime aids the cause. And in addition to denying the other side a possession, you send the other team to the locker room on a down note. It is an opportunity for advantage.

Finally, what about trotting out the "Hack-a-Shaq" strategy at the end of the period to generate an extra possession, even if the other team is in the bonus? This strategy is addressed more fully in chapter 6, with respect to long-term comebacks, but is it relevant here. The Hack-a-Shaq strategy can rob the opposition of a possession. The assumption is that the fouled player will make only one or neither of their two shots and your team will likely score at the other end to close out the period.

THE DWINDLING SHOT CLOCK MOMENT

While not an end-of-the quarter moment, the dwindling shot clock situation presents similar considerations and an opportunity to take away a possession from the opposition. Teams facing a shot clock violation get anxious, and the smarter ones will try to lure the defense into mistakes as their window of opportunity begins to close. A team defending in this situation needs to up the intelligence ante and understand they are holding the cards.

First, defenders should stay down on shooters, be ready for shot fakes, and avoid trying to block shots. Smart offensive players, when a shot clock violation looms, will lure defenders into contact with shot fakes or off-balance shots.

Second, to further eliminate offensive options, on your "call" from the bench, deny pass receivers the ball or, more ambitiously, trap. If practiced enough, the defense can surprise the offense by making passing more difficult or overwhelming the ball handler and inducing panic.

Third, rebounders should be especially alert for the wild shot. To avoid the shot clock violation, the offense will sometimes toss up a shot more designed to draw iron than score, in hopes of an offensive rebound and new possession. The interior players, in particular, must be aware of the path of the ball to maximize chances of a defensive rebound. This is an opportunity to take away a possession. Add a specific defensive call to trigger a strategy, for example, a trap, at a specific moment or at least to remind players to be especially prudent and careful. See appendix B.

The end of quarters and first-half situations are worthy of special treatment. They recur from game to game and provide important opportunities.

5

PROTECTING A SIZABLE LEAD: A LONG-TERM GAME STRATEGY

"We can't win at home. We can't win on the road. As general manager, I just can't figure out where else to play."—Pat Williams

After three quarters, we are up 12 against a talented and well-coached team. I feel a major run coming that will emphasize perimeter shooting. Last year, with a senior-laden team, I sat tight in these situations. This year, my young team needs hands-on management—often. Sure enough, on the next possession, laxity allows a three. I call a timeout to make two adjustments.

I tell the team to run our motion offense, with a minimum of five passes per possession and shots limited to finishes off penetration and drive and kick to the perimeter. Defensively, I tell them to switch everything—the other team loves ball screens—and on the switch, to jump out at ball handlers (vertical switching) to foil quick shots off screens. I tell wing defenders to show and not help on penetration, staying relatively close to perimeter shooters. We will rely on interior help defense to combat penetration.

During the next five defensive possessions, we get three stops and give up five points (a two and a three). On our corresponding offensive possessions, we get to the foul line three times (and go 4-for-6) and miss two decent shots. At the 4:10 mark, we are up by eight, and I call a timeout again. I first affirm the great job the boys have done. We will stay with the same offensive scheme. On defense, however, since the other team has figured things out a little, we will trap ball screens on the next two possessions and thereafter switch everything.

We cause a turnover on the first trap and get a stop on the next. At the two-minute mark, we are up by 11 and coast the rest of the way for a decisive win.

Sizeable leads (10 to 20 points) when a lengthy portion of a game remains—at least one to two quarters—can rarely be presumed safe. Some teams withstand runs and close well; others struggle here and there, and stagger to the finish line, barely escaping with the win; and others still wilt under pressure and end up losing. Consistency, good or bad, in this situation implies the existence of inherent player DNA, reflecting the degree of innate poise and mental toughness. But even so, coaches can make a difference when the glare of victory beams at the end of the tunnel and the team needs a little help getting there.

AN INITIAL DOSE OF REALITY: TO ADJUST OR NOT ADJUST

The initial question is whether to fiddle with whatever bestowed the seemingly comfortable lead. Overcoaching, often the product of anxiety, is risky. When the team has a nice flow, tinkering can be counterproductive. For example, staying with a hot shooter or scorer, or successful defenses and offensive sets, the tried and true, seems sensible. The simple approach is to emphasize stops and let the offense continue unimpeded.

What if, however, your team has a past pattern of allowing leads to evaporate and ceding control of the game to other teams? No matter how well they have played while building the lead, realistic expectations are what produce effective strategies. When the seasonal journey starts, coaches commonly have short-term and long-term expectations for their teams. As the season evolves, however, coaches can benefit from a reevaluation of early expectations. Reassessing—and often adjusting—expectations improves coaching effectiveness (and reduces coaching frustration). Standing pat, in contrast, often means having expectations beyond what teams can deliver. Knowing your team well and being honest about what they can and cannot do can help the team navigate the challenges of staying in front and closing with a W. If you feel adjustments are warranted, the following are some considerations from both sides of the halfcourt line.

DEFENSIVE CONSIDERATIONS

The Reminders Timeout

Consider calling a relatively early timeout to remind your players of a few things. Paramount in this situation is a keen focus on getting stops. Defensive pressure, particularly if your team's foul count is low, can stymie a catch-up strategy and, better yet, generate a turnover or two, which in this situation is gold. If your opposition is in the bonus or about to be, however, remind players that the other team will try to fool them into fouls, and in that regard, stress team communication and defensive fundamentals; for example, playing defense with the feet (not hands) and staying down on shooters (not taking shot-fake bait). Also remind them to refrain from blocking three-point attempts and instead close out shooters with the stutter step, as drilled in practice.

Their defensive job is to lower the percentage likelihood of the perimeter shot, not block it. Underscore the importance of keeping dribblers out of the lane and staying in front of ball handlers. And alert them to how the other side might try to narrow the gap with a press, a halfcourt trap, transition, or an old-school three-point play, as well as by attacking the basket looking for contact and so forth. These may seem obvious and second nature, but teams need to refocus during competition. Finally, be positive in words and tone; victory is around the corner.

Specific Adjustments

If you sense an impending surge of momentum against your team or believe for whatever reason that you must slow things down to decrease possessions and increase the percentage of the shots your team takes, be prepared to implement a specific strategy. If, for example, the other team wants to push the ball, you can contest the outlet pass or deny or match up with the outlet receiver and make filling lanes more difficult to slow them down. You can, as discussed in the prior chapter, use substitutions to halt and slow down the game before the other team can enter the ball after a make. Forcing the other team to spend clock time dealing with what you throw at them will impede their catch-up plan.

Consider mixing up defenses to confuse and force adjustments, assuming your team is comfortable moving from one defense to another. For instance, on a make (field goal or foul shot), retreat into a zone, and on a miss, match up and play man defense. Generally speaking, a well-implemented zone forces the offensive team to use more clock than man defense. Of course, the zone has risks. Be mindful of both three-point shooters and the need to pack the paint to prevent penetration, two goals that can conflict. Moreover, have in mind the actual performance history of your zone defense and, in particular, its ability to match up with spot-up shooters on ball reversal. Weigh the probabilities based on past performance. Be realistic. And know your opponent.

Alternatively, on a make, apply full-court ball pressure to slow the offense down as they bring the ball up the floor, and cause them to start their offense in less desirable halfcourt spots. You can employ this strategy after a timeout as well (as discussed in chapter 1). Similarly, a soft or containment press that does not seek to create turnovers—and thus is less risky—will slow down the game as well. Force the other team to use clock and keep the ball out of the middle of the floor.

Do you keep or pull a press you have used successfully for the entire game? That is a tough question, and the answer draws heavily from personnel assessment. On the one hand, unless your team has begun to lose focus with the press or the other team has figured it out, its continuation seems logical. On the other hand, a press, by definition, presents risks. Coaches stay in presses mainly because the long-term benefits outweigh the long-term risks. On the other hand, this may not be the time to take risks, especially if you believe your team can handle the challenge of closing out a game with a lead. If inclined to stay with the press, monitor each possession for signs of unfocused play. At the first sign of slippage, intercede, regroup your players, and, if necessary, change the approach. Doubt can be a slippery slope toward fear and then panic.

The Fouling Game

Finally, if the other team has elected to foul to stop the clock and force you to make foul shots, have a good foul-shooting team on the floor, as discussed in chapter 2. Keep the ball in the hands of your best free-throw shooters as much as practicable and away from players whose track record at the line is wanting.

OFFENSIVE CONSIDERATIONS

On the other side of the ball, lead protection places a premium on time management and excellent offensive possessions. Hall of Fame coach Al McGuire captured this situation succinctly: "The clock is now your enemy." The other team wants to extend the game and generate extra possessions to fuel their catch-up plan. A bad possession for your team is the equivalent of a turnover. Consider, then, a rule about what shots may be taken and when. For example, you might allow shots at the rim at any time during the shot clock and all other shots only in rhythm of the offense or with less than 15 seconds on shot clock, or some variation. You can also impose a minimum touch or pass requirement, say four to six passes minimum, or require that both sides of the floor get touches. Whatever the specific adjustments, seek to impose discipline. Practice this situation so it becomes familiar ground.

In jurisdictions without a shot clock, think twice about freezing the ball, which could take your team out of its comfort zone, breed tentativeness, and cause turnovers or bad shot selection. Instead, use the clock effectively to create high-percentage shots.

Finally, be alert to call timeout to retain possession to avoid a five-second call or held-ball whistle (unless the possession arrow pointing is your way). As emphasized, make sure your players know which team has the possession arrow and who is authorized to call timeouts in this situation.

❈ ❈ ❈

Protecting a lead is a team skill honed in practice. Losing after enjoying a commanding lead is demoralizing and can have a long-term negative impact, especially if repeated. Practicing these situations provides teams with familiarity of game dynamics, including time management and decision making, and builds confidence. If a team develops insecure tendencies in these situations, they can tumble down a negative path from which return is difficult. The more this situation is practiced, the less likely teams will be to stammer and surrender significant leads.

6

CATCH-UP SITUATIONS AND THE LONG-TERM COMEBACK STRATEGY

"I was thinking about making a comeback until I pulled a muscle vacuuming."—Johnny Bench

We are in a single-elimination postseason game against a team we beat by 21 earlier in the season in a nonleague game, to the surprise of many. It doesn't take long to realize this higher-stakes game will be different. With four minutes left in the second quarter, we are down 16, and the floor dynamics are anything but encouraging. I normally would let things play out for the last few minutes of the half and ponder major changes at the break. This time, however, I harbor great doubt we can turn it around without a major adjustment right now. I call timeout and change our defense from man to an aggressive matchup zone.

The new defense confuses the other team and infuses ours with energy. At halftime, we are down 10. After the break, we play them even for a while, and after three quarters, the spread is eight. We steadily wear them down and build momentum. With two minutes left, we are down two. In the next 90 seconds, we trade stops and baskets, and then, on a dead ball, as the other team is about to have a possession up two with 33 seconds left, I call timeout. We switch to man defense, and I direct that if we get a possession off a stop, to attack full court without delay. We get the stop at six seconds. I don't call timeout—their defense is, as hoped, disorganized—and we charge down the floor, getting get a good look at a 20-foot buzzer-

beater shot that rolls around—for an eternity—and, finally and ex-
cruciatingly, off the rim. We lose by two, and our season ends.

The severe disappointment of the loss aside, I do not believe we
would have had the chance to tie the game if I had waited until later,
as I normally would have, to make the major adjustment. Changing
the defense in the second quarter gave us the time to close the gap
steadily and put us in position to win. Perhaps if we had started even
earlier . . .

The successful comeback is one of the most thrilling experiences in
sports. While no team wants to find itself in a situation where a favorable game outcome requires a major comeback, virtually every team in
every sport must at one time or another confront the often-formidable
challenge of a come-from-behind victory. Succeeding against the odds
instills in players and coaches alike a belief in the possibilities and the
power of achievement. It also pays homage to the oft-stated colloquial-
ism, "It ain't over till the fat lady sings," or if you prefer the charming
utterances of the late Yogi Berra, "It ain't over until it's over" (and it
wasn't, as the Mets eliminated a nine-and-a-half-game deficit in July
1973, to win the National League East divisional title).

THE PSYCHOLOGY OF THE COMEBACK

The odds of pulling off this reversal of fortune essentially turn on three
things: 1) foremost, the ability of your team to gain consistent stops on
defense; 2) how prepared your team is to implement a comeback strategy, including how patient and disciplined they are; and 3) how much the
team genuinely believes they will emerge victorious.

The first is self-evident. The second is informed by how much time
you devote to this situation in practice. The third warrants comment.
Coaches who exhibit genuine confidence have significant influence on
their teams. Players feed off coaching energy and demeanor in stressful
times. A confident coach breeds player confidence, and a nervous coach
breeds eagerness about impending doom. Positive affirmations about
prospects and belief in the team, especially when the intensity of the
game is at an apex, are sometimes as important as Xs and Os. This
includes body language, which speaks volumes about what we feel.

Similarly, more "dos" than "don'ts" convey a positive sense of the mission rather than fear about what to avoid.

As discussed in the prior chapter, be realistic about what you can expect from your players, especially in this context. We naturally resist the temptation to believe our team lacks mental toughness, cannot withstand the heat of a pressure-filled game situation, or has a tendency to succumb to the powerful grip of the fear of failure. But what are their patterns? How have they responded in the past? Have you worked enough on stressful game situations in practice to make players sufficiently comfortable in games? Your team will have a track record that discloses how they tend to respond to adversity. Use realistic expectations to formulate strategy and determine what they need from you to succeed.

THE TIMING OF THE COMEBACK STRATEGY

The difficult threshold question is *when* to launch a comeback plan. While there is certainly no ready-made, bright line on the clock, timing is material. Making significant changes often introduces new risks. If you start too early and the risks materialize at the get-go, you are set back further. If you wait, hoping for a natural sequence of advantages and benefits, you risk, even if the team performs admirably, running out of time. How many times have you heard a coach lament, "We simply ran out of time"?

This timing continuum raises various questions. For example, how many points must your team be behind before you embark on a formulated comeback trail? How much time must be on the clock? What if you are behind 20 in the first half or midway through the third quarter? Do you do anything special at that time? What must the deficit be entering the fourth quarter to introduce a specifically designed comeback strategy? Does it have to be double digits or greater?

Many coaches initially stand pat in these situations, but unless your team cannot chip away steadily in the normal flow to bring the contest within reach in time to close the game strong, a delayed decision can cost the team any real chance to turn things around.

Coaches can be seduced by the allure of withholding radical action in the hope their team can deliver a string of defensive stops and points on the board, a dream combination. We all know situations where teams perform a virtual miracle by making up enormous ground in relatively little time. The *30 for 30* documentary "Winning Time" features one of the most famous: Reggie Miller of the Indiana Pacers putting up eight points in the last 18.7 seconds of the fourth quarter to shock the Knicks in the second game of the 1995 Eastern Conference Semifinals. There are many examples of teams making up 20-plus points in a quarter or similar runs to pull off a stunning come-from-behind victory. Recall, for instance, the Stephen Curry–led Golden State Warrior overtime victory against the New Orleans Pelicans in the third game of the first round of the 2015 NBA Western Conference playoffs after being down by 20 to start the fourth quarter and 17 with six minutes left in regulation.

But these accomplishments represent the world of the improbable. While it would be nice to have a Reggie Miller or Stephen Curry clone lying in wait to foster a miracle, wise coaching decisions deal—or should deal—with probabilities.

For example, assume you are down 10 entering the fourth quarter with eight minutes to go. This seems manageable on the surface, and you might instinctively believe specialized action is premature. After all, in two possessions, you could conceivably close the gap to six or even four, and if that happens, you are back in the saddle. But is it really premature? As time passes, the importance of each possession in this situation magnifies. In the proverbial blink of an eye, the opposite can occur and you could find yourself down 12 or more with six minutes left—and have lost both precious ground and time.

Return to a set of familiar queries: What do you see in your players in the moment? Are they getting rattled? Are they steady and confident? What is their history in these situations? Also be mindful of how many possessions are likely available. The overriding goal in a comeback journey is to increase possessions. To state the obvious, the more chances you have and the fewer your opponent has to score improves the odds of reducing the point gap and winning the game. While it is difficult to know the minimum number of possessions left in a game, you can get a general sense; as discussed in chapter 7, you may want to assume an average of 23 seconds a possession for planning purposes.

TIMEOUTS ALONG THE COMEBACK TRAIL

Strategic use of timeouts is integral to the comeback strategy. If you are successful in catching up and you can tie the game or make it a one- or two-possession game, you likely will need timeouts in crunch time. Again, you will probably need to use a timeout to discuss the overall comeback strategy and give reminders. Whether you use additional timeouts down the road is a judgment call that balances how acute the need to talk to your players against the projected need to retain timeouts for the end of the game. And lest we forget, there is always the possibility of overtime. This can be a fluid situation, requiring constant reassessment.

THE COMEBACK STRATEGY: WHAT TO CONSIDER ON OFFENSE

The offensive component of a comeback strategy must be narrowly defined. It is vital that your players have a particular focus on the offensive end. The goal should be to take high-percentage shots in the least amount of time and extend the game by stopping the clock as often as possible. This is not to say you should avoid three-point shot opportunities. A three-point shot can be a high-percentage take for some players in certain moments; for instance, in the rhythm of your offense. Indeed, a trey or more can do wonders for a comeback. Generally, however, the most sound strategy is to attack the basket—using two-foot stops—to draw fouls, stop the clock, seek old-school three-point plays, and extend the game. Again, the longer the game, the more possessions and the better the chances of a successful comeback.

Stress patience in the halfcourt offense and good decisions with the ball. Both are generally hard enough for many teams, never mind when players are eager to make up lots of ground as time slips way. Nonetheless, more than ever, a deliberate and focused halfcourt attack that makes the defense work is conducive to getting the high-percentage shot that may be your ticket to a successful comeback. And while, as noted, three-point shots can be perfectly fine in the rhythm of your offense, jacking up threes to secure the proverbial "three-run homer" plays into the hands of the other team and will likely worsen the situation.

Poise goes a long way here as well. A major hurdle to overcome in many comebacks is execution perfection. A comeback run can ill afford too many mistakes. Execution errors that may not seem momentous during the normal course of the game take on a distinctly different significance when trying to close a gap with time running out. Poise breeds sound decision making, and a patient team is well suited for the resurgence battle. And, yes, these qualities are more likely to emerge in real time if you devote practice time to comeback situations.

Another tempting strategy is to push the ball, whether off a make or a miss, or both. The advantage is the opportunity to score in limited seconds, provided good decisions are made, increasing the potential for more possessions. The risk is committing turnovers and losing possessions if the quickness and energy of the transition game are mishandled and produce bad decisions with the ball. A team that has practiced adhering to sound fast-break principles should be able to extend the game with quicker scores. Heed the words of John Wooden: "Be quick, but don't hurry." Moreover, be mindful of the fatigue factor. It is important to have fresh legs on the floor. Fatigue can foil a comeback strategy.

Finally, offensive rebounding strategy is essential in this situation. Teams vary in their rebounding systems on offense. Some send three to the glass and have two back for defensive balance. Some send four with one back, and still some, who do not fear the risk of transition, send five. The downside of sending many to the glass is transition risk, and you have to assess, all things considered, including time on the clock and the score differential, whether the added risk is worth the extra dedication of bodies to the glass. If the risk is too great, send four and keep a sole defender back. However you choose to handle the scenario, you will likely need to increase second-chance opportunities through more effective rebounding.

THE COMEBACK STRATEGY: WHAT TO CONSIDER ON DEFENSE

The goal of any defensive part of the comeback strategy is straightforward: Secure the basketball either with stops or turnovers. To succeed, a change in energy and hustle is necessary. The mental quotient of the game must change. The greater the energy, the more rattled the other team might become. Escalating verbalization, effective among teammates, can intimidate the other team and reset the tone. Take the game to the offense, not the reverse, and force the other team into mistakes.

Once again, most players need reminders, both in timeouts and from the bench during play, about such select defensive fundamentals as staying in front of dribblers, playing defense with their feet and refraining from reaching, staying down on shooters and not committing "fly-bys" against three-point shooters, keeping their arms straight up when defending the interior shot ("verticality"), and communicating help and screen defense.

The turnover part is naturally more complicated. Pressing and trapping defenses can be invaluable tools in the comeback. They force turnovers or at least poor shot selection, especially early in the shot clock. Pressure and traps also precipitate poor decisions by forcing the other players to get caught up in an accelerated tempo and rush things. Pressure defense also, of course, involves risk, particularly in the overloads and rotations that occur when two people trap. At some point, however, especially if time has become the major factor or your team is not getting consistent halfcourt stops, you may have to go this route. If disinclined to press or trap, however, consider full-court ball pressure, which can tax the main ball handler, disrupt the pace of the other team's offense, and possibly force bad decisions.

FOUL STRATEGY DURING THE COMEBACK

Finally, there is the foul strategy. This is covered in chapter 2 but needs brief mention here. Foul only for advantage, know who to foul when you need to foul, and remind players to make a strong play on the ball for a possible steal and avoid the intentional foul call.

And what about the Hack-a-Shaq strategy? It is, at first, the quintessential probability strategy in come-from-behind situations. While it has become controversial, it can work. The strategy assumes that, during the course of its implementation, the target of the foul will produce fewer points per possession from the foul line than their team would in the normal course of its offense. The strategy also stops the clock and extends the game.

But there are countervailing considerations. The foul shooter might rise to the occasion and foil the strategy, the main risk. Furthermore, it increases team fouls and accelerates putting the other team in the bonus. More subtly, it implies a lack of confidence in your team's ability to get consistent stops or generate turnovers. The strategy also disrupts the rhythm of the game and could deflate defensive energy. Finally, the Hack-a-Shaq foul is "intentional," and teams, especially in high school, must be keyed to any applicable rules that have negative consequences for away-from-the-ball fouls.

✿ ✿ ✿

The comeback can be an exhilarating ride that tests the mettle of coaches and players alike. A successful jaunt down the comeback trail builds long-term confidence and becomes part of what teammates and coaches forever share with one another.

7

END-OF-THE-GAME SITUATIONS (MINIMAL POSSESSIONS LEFT)

"If you don't know where you are going, you might wind up someplace else."—Yogi Berra

The last time we played this team, we trailed by 10 with four minutes to go and decided not to give fouls until the two-minute mark. It proved too little, too late. I promised myself that if the situation repeated itself, I would start fouling earlier. It has. This time, we are down nine against the same team with 3:20 left. I call timeout, and as our team comes off the floor, I review with my staff our list of opposing poor foul shooters. I tell the team to foul on each possession until I say differently. As expected, they protest; they want to play straight up. I hate overruling them, but I do not think we can win otherwise and do not waver.

During the next two minutes, we put the other team on the line four times for one-and-one situations. They miss the front end twice and make two of the other four. In our corresponding possessions, we register seven points and cut the gap to four with 1:15 on the clock. I call timeout and remove the intentional-foul strategy. We get a stop and a score on the next two possessions, putting us in a one-possession game with 27 seconds to go and on defense. We elect not to foul but to trap the second pass at halfcourt, which we have not done throughout the entire game. This surprises the other team and causes a travel. We have the ball with the chance to tie or win. We elect to go for the tie and force overtime, and are successful. And while we struggle in the extra frame, we miraculously eke out a one-point win when the other team makes a crucial mental error on their last possession.

The end of a game tests the game management skills of coaches perhaps more than any other situation, as it challenges coaches to put players in specific positions to win. This chapter addresses situations where minimal possessions remain in the game, and the next (chapter 8) addresses situations where teams face a presumed final possession.

The pressure to make wise game decisions when the game is on the line is plain enough, but it reveals a different quality when you consider that these situations play out in unpredictable ways, making it difficult to anticipate every conceivable scenario. Time on the clock, the score, number of possessions left, foul counts, matchups, and personnel, among other things, converge to render crunch-time decisions as high art. Nonetheless, repeated advance preparation and an emphasis on instilling good habits help players execute with precision and confidence when the game is on the line. Said John Wooden, "Failing to prepare is preparing to fail."

WHAT IS YOUR END-OF-GAME SYSTEM?

Teams are advantaged if they have a set of rules and expectations that frame strategy in these situations. For example:

- What is the established minimum clock time for implementing your 2-for-1 set (see chapter 4)?
- Who inbounds the ball at the opposite basket when the other team is looking for a steal?
- Who inbounds the ball under your basket when a game-winning shot is needed?
- Who is on the floor when the other team is going to foul?
- Who is on the short list to take the final shot of a game?
- Who is on the floor when a stop or steal is needed?
- Who on the floor tracks shot and game clock seconds?

Assistant coaches play a pivotal role here. Head coaches understandably get caught up in the moments of close games. Assigning an assistant coach to deliver reminders will make crunch-time decisions more effective. This might include 1) identifying players to foul in order of foul-shooting weakness; 2) alerting officials of your intention to call timeout after a make, give a foul, or call timeout if you cannot inbound the ball within five seconds; 3) reminding inbounds passers that they may run the baseline after a make; or 4) identifying the players who can execute the full-court pass when necessary.

The value of planning, including allocation of responsibility among the coaching staff, again, cannot be underestimated. As you review the discussion of specifics that follows, consider how you might construct a suitable system for various late-game situations.

MINIMAL POSSESSIONS LEFT: GENERAL CONSIDERATIONS

The prior two chapters discuss protecting leads and making comebacks using a long-term strategy. Here, we look at the more immediate and short-term situation: crunch time. When "crunch time" begins varies, although generally speaking, it is often the final three to five minutes of a two-possession game (four to six points). The model used here, for purposes of analysis, is when three minutes or less remain in a three-possession game when behind, ahead, and tied.

Some coaches prefer to go toe-to-toe in this situation on a possession-by-possession basis, content in the belief their team can take care of business as usual. This approach handicaps the odds of success based on confidence in personnel and style of play, among other possible factors, and avoids major adjustments. It can be effective.

Another approach is exerting greater control to increase perceived probabilities of success. As noted, many factors influence close games. Each of the main factors—the score, likely possessions left, the foul situation, and, of course, available game time—constantly changes, and as each does, outcome probabilities shift, prompting the need to reassess and possibly readjust to better the odds of success.

The likely number of remaining possessions is a key probability factor. A commonly accepted formula for determining possessions per game is: possessions = field goals attempted + .475 of free throw attempts − offensive rebounds + turnovers. Applying this formula to a modest sampling of high school game statistics, I estimated that the average time of possession is 23 seconds. Based on this estimate, three minutes, or 180 seconds, produce a minimum of eight possessions, four for each team. More possessions obviously can occur, and the balance of possessions can shift favorably to one team, especially if time of possession down the stretch tightens, as it can do. But a working assumption of 23 seconds per possession provides a fair starting point for discussion and underscores that with three minutes left in the game, for strategic purposes, a team cannot assume more than four to six possessions. See appendix F.

For example, if behind in a nine-point or full three-possession game, even if you optimistically assume both teams have six offensive possessions available at the three-minute mark, and even if your team gets stops every time—a worthy goal that is possible but not probable from a planning standpoint—to close the gap, your team must put up nine points in six possessions, an ambitious project. This underscores the difficulty of winning in this situation without making specific adjustments to increase team possessions.

The particulars of the aforementioned hypothetical are designed to provoke thought and provide a planning framework. The underlying numerical assumptions can, of course, differ in game situations. Changing the number of possessions, adding time to the clock, and changing the lead differential contemplate variables in real-time situations. They do not, however, alter the overarching goal: increasing probability of success. The circumstances of the last few minutes of a relatively close game are dynamic, and coaches must be attentive to how they change. Limiting focus to each possession as it comes can be, well, shortsighted. A more effective approach, it seems, is to peer down the road and take a snapshot of what you are realistically able to do with what possessions are available.

MINIMAL POSSESSIONS LEFT: WHEN BEHIND

As noted, if behind three possessions with about three minutes left in the game, coaches sometimes elect to play without major adjustments, hoping the team will generate a score-stop pattern. Making up nine points in three minutes to close out a game, while ambitious, can happen. To maximize the chances this approach can succeed, however, a team must steadily whittle away the lead. Trading baskets early in this effort will substantially decrease the odds of success.

If inclined to adjust, there are many common adjustments to consider: pressing and trapping on defense, pushing the ball on offense looking for quick baskets, and getting more aggressive on the glass. Furthermore, as discussed earlier, attacking the rim smartly and drawing contact on the finish can do wonders for the short-term comeback by putting points on the board, stopping the clock, and adding fouls to the other team. There is also the three-point shooting attack if you have enough perimeter shooters who know when to take the three-point shot. Some teams have a three-point shooting "team" for this specific situation and specific offensive sets to free their shooters, for example, the dribble-drive offense.

Underscore to players the value of good shot selection, which is often tested with the game on the line. Bad shot selection, an unrecorded turnover, can be a rally killer. This again is where practice comes in handy. Players need to learn good habits, including discipline in tough moments, through a regimen of special situational practice. And while potentially controversial, benching a starter who has a tendency to hog the ball and jack up hero shots can mean the difference in game outcome (although it likely will add to your postgame drama agenda).

One option many coaches seldom elect to use is the early implementation of the intentional foul, as recounted in the opening scenario. Many coaches prefer to delay the intentional foul until late in the game. Teams that wait, however, often find themselves in a game of two or more possessions with a minute or so to go, rendering the intentional fouling strategy more hopeful than practical. Consider, instead, starting the process with about three minutes to go if behind three possessions, especially if the other team has one or two relatively poor foul shooters on the floor. While the offense may try to keep the ball away from poor foul shooters, a fouling strategy that starts early allows you to wait longer in given possessions to isolate poor foul shooters. You can, for example, have the defender guarding the poor foul shooter double-team the ball, making the poor foul shooter the "habit" pass receiver out of the trap, where the foul can be given. The defensive rotations in this strategy are key and must be well-practiced.

If you cannot bridge the gap and are still behind three possessions or double digits with less than two minutes left, you have to pull out all the stops. While miracles do happen, you cannot expect one. You must take risk by having players overplay and flash passing lanes looking for steals, double-team, and trap, and, again, make judicious use of the three-point shot. You can also leak a player for a transition opportunity and a quick score. Once again, poise, both among the coaching staff and players, should be a constant no matter what strategy you employ.

If you play in a system without a shot clock and face a stall game when behind, you have to ask (and likely keep asking) an essential question: Do you foul and risk points to get the ball? The answer depends on how far you are behind and how much time is left. Waiting to foul is a good idea if you have sufficient time to try to force a turnover. If, however, you need to make up substantial points, this situation is not much different than if operating with a shot clock. You need to foul, stop the clock, and hopefully trade one for two points a few times or more. Of course, the other team might place all their good foul shooters on the floor, especially in a stall game, where there is a premium on skilled ball handlers who tend to be the better foul shooters. Either way, you cannot sit idle for long.

MINIMAL POSSESSIONS LEFT: WHEN AHEAD

When ahead with three minutes or so on the clock, the essential strategy should be to focus on getting productive offensive and defensive possessions without making major adjustments and extend the status quo to the buzzer. Still, there are specific considerations.

First, a timeout in this situation, even if your team seems to have things well in hand, can enhance chances of success. At the risk of belaboring a point, players need reminders, and things can go south fast, especially if you suffer a couple of consecutive bad possessions. While all coaches want their players to close well without their help—to build confidence and reap long-term rewards—a timeout can affirm team performance and provide discrete reminders to ensure everyone is on the same page. Similarly, your team is likely to see pressure. If you can anticipate when it might arrive, a timeout to discuss how to handle it is beneficial. You also might want your better ball handlers in the game to help weather the anticipated pressure storm.

Second, the other team, especially if enjoying the bonus, will seek to close the gap by attacking the basket and getting to the line. Nursing a lead with three minutes left must take this risk into account. It is an opportunity to reassess who is on the floor and what defensive reminders you give them. Do you want your best defensive unit in the game, including players who are not foul prone?

Third, effective clock management on offense is essential. To state the obvious, the more time your team uses, the harder the other team has to work on defense and the less time it has for its offense, making catching up more difficult. This does not mean holding the ball for the sake of holding the ball; rather, it means using the clock wisely and looking for high-percentage shots. This situation deserves meaningful attention in practice so players are comfortable with how to run the offense when ahead.

Fourth, second-chance opportunities hold special importance here too. Using clock twice in a single possession as a result of an offensive rebound reduces possessions for the other side and exhausts valuable clock time. It can also demoralize an opponent. Consider a specific strategy to attack the glass for second chances when ahead in this situation, including how to minimize over-the-back calls and the risk of transition offense.

Finally, in systems with no shot clock, the consideration is whether to hold the ball and freeze the other side out of possessions. This is a sensitive decision because a stall can take your team out of its basic offense. Will your players be tentative and overly cautious? If you deploy a stall too early, will you risk loss of momentum? How much time have you spent practicing this approach? How long can your players sustain this strategy effectively? A slow-tempo team will, in theory at least, be better equipped to hold the ball because it blends with their natural style of play and identity. An uptempo team may not respond as seamlessly.

How do you implement? Do you allow any shots at all? What about uncontested layups? If so, do you require a minimum number of touches before allowing a shot? Again, whatever your preferences, successful implementation depends in large measure on ample time devoted in practice to your approach. Like the come-from-behind situation, skillful offensive execution, including good shot selection, can foil any comeback attempt.

MINIMAL POSSESSIONS LEFT: TIE GAMES

Tie games with three minutes to go generally do not call up in-depth strategic challenges. At first blush, the essential strategy is to play well at both ends of the floor. This is not to say that coaches should not make adjustments to try to alter the balance of power in the game, only that tie games in crunch time do not scream out for a major adjustment as a general proposition, except perhaps where one team has caught up with a major run and has significant momentum.

Tie games get interesting, however, under two minutes, as you quickly approach a literal possession versus possession battle. Assume, for example, a tie game with 52 seconds left and your team has the ball. This situation, in theory, implicates your 2-for-1 set (see chapter 4). If you have a quick hitter that can get you a great shot in, say, 10 seconds, a make gives the ball to the other side with 42 seconds on the clock and virtually guarantees you another possession.

But do you want to deploy a 2-for-1 strategy here? Is a 2-for-1 plan risky, insofar as it imposes too much pressure on your players to take a shot in sufficient time to ensure you will get another possession? As discussed in chapter 4, some coaches are disinclined to use the 2-for-1 at the end of games, preferring their team to focus on getting a great shot rather an early shot and avoid putting the team in a situation where player attention might be divided between two potentially conflicting objectives: a quality shot and a relatively quick shot.

On the other hand, if the clock shows 52 seconds at the start of the possession and your team takes 20 to 25 seconds to score, the shot clock is off and the opponent has the opportunity to tie or take the lead, leaving your team minimal, if any, opportunity for another possession. In that case, you are playing the odds your team will get a stop.

What is the best strategy for your team? The value of the possession is paramount, no matter how you choose to run the offense. It could be the last chance you have to score. Seeking your cake and eating it too, by trying to tease two possessions out of this situation, while not unreasonable, is bold and risky.

Assume that, instead of having the ball in a tied game, you are defending and both teams are in the bonus. At first blush, this seems easy. You defend for the stop, and if all goes well, you might get the last possession and an opportunity to win. Any abrupt changes might be disruptive. There are, however, certain things to consider.

Do you change defenses to mix things up? Do you, for example, zone the other team, especially if you have played man for most or all of the game? Alternatively, consider slightly tweaking your man-to-man defense to a "switching defense," either "guards-to-guards" or "bigs-to-bigs," or by switching everyone (and accepting the mismatches). This can disrupt the other team, especially coming out of a timeout.

Do you trap to force a turnover? Do you apply ball pressure as the ball comes up the floor to use clock and force them to initiate their halfcourt set other than where they prefer?

As with questions in other contexts, the answers lie in player assessment, the familiarity of the situation through practice, and your own comfort with specific approaches. In the end, what are the relative success probabilities of available approaches?

✿ ✿ ✿

The last few minutes of a game can be fluid, requiring continuous reassessment. While many suggestions in this chapter may seem obvious, at least from 30,000 feet, refocusing on these situations through a vigorous practice regimen, constant reminders to players, and a portfolio of strategic tools is a world apart from theoretical knowledge. We coaches can never spend enough time reviewing the range of challenges games offer and how to respond to them, and inspiring our players in the process. Said Dr. Jack Ramsay, "Players draw confidence from a poised, alert coach who anticipates changes in game conditions."

8

END-OF-THE-GAME SITUATIONS (FINAL POSSESSIONS)

"If you meet the Buddha in the lane, feed him the ball."—Phil Jackson

I always suffer an extra dose of worry when facing an overachieving and well-coached team in their gym. Those teams do all the little things well to make up for lesser talent, which is precisely the kind of team we now face in an important league game. To complicate matters, we have recently struggled and need a W to keep our favorable playoff seeding.

As dreaded, the game is a struggle. We start off slow and fall behind by six after the first quarter. We rally, however, and take a one-point lead into halftime. The rest of the game is back and forth, and with 45 seconds left in the contest, we score to bring us within one point. I call timeout, my third of the game, leaving me two. I keep things optimistically simple: Do not foul, get a stop, come down the floor, run the offense with patience, score, and win.

We get the stop and bring the ball down. When we cross half-court, I decide to call timeout, leaving me one. I tell them to attack the basket off a screen and roll-based offensive set we sometimes use. We get good spacing and score off a baseline roll with three seconds left, giving us a one-point lead. The team is celebrating and not paying attention to the other team. For my part, I assume the clock will run out, but when I look up, I see it is frozen at three seconds, which means the home scorekeeper has stopped the clock impermissibly. As I bring my eyes down, I see an opposing player grab the ball out of the net and—with the clock not moving in the moment—throw a baseball pass to a teammate running down the floor, who catches the rock, dribbles, and scores at the buzzer. My protest to the referee falls on deaf ears. But, more important, I realize my double failure to instruct the players during the timeout on what to do if we score and to call my final timeout to set up our full-court defense are the bigger problems. Lessons learned.

This chapter discusses the final possession situation in tied games, when ahead, and when behind. Here, "final possession" means when the shot clock is off, even though additional possessions might occur (and present new strategic considerations). For analytical purposes, however, using a final-possession framework where a shot clock violation is not a risk presents the essential dynamics for managing the last 30 or 35 seconds of a game.

GENERAL CLOCK MANAGEMENT

Teams need to learn that clock management often means playing differently than how they played for most of the game. For example, when ahead, it might be better to slow down and set up the halfcourt offense after a defensive rebound and run clock rather than trying to convert a possible transition basket. The former reflects smart clock management, and the latter is better suited for earlier in the game when other considerations prevail. Thus, a set of expectations is important when managing clock during the last possession:

- How much time do you want on the clock when taking the shot?
- Do you allow for the possibility of an offensive rebound?
- Do you prefer instead to take the last shot at or near the buzzer and forgo any second-chance opportunity?
- What offensive sets are designed for this situation?
- What defense do you prefer to set up?

The timing of fouls-to-give on defense is equally sensitive. For example, if behind by two with the shot clock off and defending, with the other team in the bonus, unless blessed with a timely turnover, you have to foul. Generally, the less time left, the sooner you foul, and the more time, the longer you might indulge temptation to wait for the often-elusive turnover. Some coaches foul at the first chance, wanting as much clock time for the next possession, while others might wait to foul—perhaps a pass or two—to see if the team can cause a turnover or until the team can foul a poor free-throw shooter. While the temptation to let your defense hunker down is tantalizing, waiting is risky. Time is precious and fading.

The essential question is, What is the least amount of time you want on the clock before committing the foul? Put differently, how much time do you prefer to have at the other end of the floor for a high-percentage shot and, if necessary, a second-chance opportunity. If you wait, for instance, until 20 seconds to commit the foul and the other team makes both shots, it is now a two-possession game, and your time for one good possession, never mind two, is limited.

Because clock management in this situation is crucial, whatever your style, having established rules allows for effective decision making. As you ponder what follows, give thought to what specific rules work for your program.

LAST-POSSESSION SITUATIONS WHEN TIED

Offense

If on offense in a tied game, with the shot clock off, the desired result is obvious: Score with insufficient time remaining for the opponent to get a good scoring opportunity. The secondary goal is to force overtime. Here are some initial questions:

- Do you have a set play for this situation?
- Do you want the first good shot or prefer to wait as long as practicable for an uncontested layup or a hard drive to the basket that can draw contact?
- Do you specify who may take the shot and what shots are not permitted?
- If the possession occurred off a defensive rebound, are you comfortable giving your team the green light to take the ball up the

floor to try to score without a timeout? In other words, have they practiced this situation sufficiently? Note: Calling timeout allows the other team to set up their goal-line stand defense, focus better on matchups, and anticipate how you might handle the last possession. It also forces you to inbound the ball, which carries turnover risk.

Revisit two key questions: How long do you hold the ball before taking the final shot and do you leave time for a second-chance opportunity? In theory, the answer to the latter question is yes, provided you do not leave so much time that on a miss the other team has a chance for a decent shot. Leaving about five seconds when your team shoots is relatively safe. This allows for a second-chance opportunity and leaves precious little time for a good offensive opportunity at the opposite end.

Add to the mix whether you are home or on the road and, if home, whether your gym means advantage in overtime. Traditional thinking is play for the tie at home and the win on the road. If you subscribe to this thinking and are at home in a tied game, you may consider taking a shot closer to the buzzer than five seconds to eliminate any chance the other side will get a possession, placing stock in overtime if you cannot convert the final shot in regulation.

What if the called play breaks down? This happens often enough in waning moments, and when it does teams can become eager, disorganized, and ill-equipped to handle departure from the plan. Do you have a backup plan? Do you call timeout (if you have one)? Do you call a different (and simpler) play, like a pick-and-roll or pop, or clear out for a strong finisher or pull-up shooter? Do you have a go-to player who has your blessing to operate freely? Do you let your point guard decide how to handle the situation? Whatever you do, think simple.

Defense

Again, when defending the last possession in a tied game, the goal is simple: Get a stop at the earliest time or, better yet, a turnover. The undesired result is putting the other team on the foul line, especially after the clock has wound down to fewer than 10 seconds. Here are some questions to ponder:

- If you are disinclined to call timeout and your opponent does not either, what defense is your team expected to get into, including how to handle screens?
- Do you have to tell them or are they prepared?
- If the ball is inbounded at the far end, do you contest the in-bounds pass, double-team the likely receiver and deny them the ball, or allow the pass?
- Do you trap, press, or fall back into your halfcourt defense?
- Do you apply full-court pressure to force the other team to use clock?
- Do you, like so many teams, allow the other team to roll the ball up the floor to delay the start of the clock? Why give them extra time when every second is dear? If you fear the ball handler can beat your defender, have your player play off enough to eliminate that risk. But force the other side to use clock at the earliest time. Make their job difficult and reduce their odds of success.

You might consider, as discussed in chapter 7, reverting to an all-switching defense to throw the other team off balance. This is an especially important consideration if a timeout is called. In a last possession, the team with the ball will likely run something specific that will include assumptions about how you will defend. An all-switching defense or some modified version can throw a monkey wrench into any well-conceived plan.

If you have fouls to give, when do you give them? This can be tricky. The other team wants to run down the clock and take the last shot of the game. Fouls-to-give can take air out that strategy by forcing an offensive reset with less time than originally planned. If playing for a tie, the challenge is picking a moment deep in the clock without fouling a shooter. If, on the other hand, you are playing for the win, the rub is leaving enough time after the make or stop for your own possession. This suggests giving the foul between 10 and 20 seconds. Alternatively, save the fouls-to-give, go for the stop, hope to score at the other end, and use the fouls-to-give as the other team desperately tries to run a play with only a few seconds left.

Finally, if you get a steal or a rebound in a tie game with the shot clock off, do you call timeout or prefer that your team come down the floor and make a play? Do they know to do that? Have they practiced this situation enough?

These questions have no preordained answers. Nonetheless, they must be asked repeatedly and dissected throughout the season to prepare coaches and players alike for these moments. Sound habits are powerful allies in pressure situations.

LAST-POSSESSION SITUATIONS WHEN BEHIND

Offense

On the offensive end, there are two situations to consider. The first is one-possession games, which includes one- and 2-point contests, as well as three-point games. The second is two-possession (or greater) games. What follows are examples of some scenarios to illustrate the various factors.

Down One or Two, with the Ball, and Enough Time to Run a Full Halfcourt Set

The threshold question is whether to play for the last shot near the end of the clock or take the quickest good shot. The risk with the former strategy is that it is all or nothing. If you miss, you are effectively done. If you strike gold, you have a dramatic win and can flash a genuine smile after the game. For sure, many coaches would elect this option.

The other approach focuses on finding a good shot as early as possible that allows time for other options if you miss. How much better a shot is likely available if you hold the ball until near the buzzer? In fact, if you wait too long, the team might get eager and force a low-percentage shot. This is not to suggest an early shot for the sake of firing one off early. As noted earlier, the goal is the best shot achievable in the least amount of time, with emphasis on the best shot. If you miss, there are options. If you get the make, you are either ahead or tied and can play for the stop with little on the clock for the other team. And, again, in this situation, in particular, consider sending at least four to the glass.

Down One or Two, with the Ball under Your Basket, and Less Than 10 Seconds to Go

In this situation, do you try to score right off the inbounds play or inbound the ball safely for a halfcourt play? Does your strategy change with a little more time to use? How much more?

First, consider installing a play that works against both man and zone defense. Second, an inbounds play designed to produce a make off the catch or a single dribble is a solid first choice. Many plays can produce this result, especially if you can anticipate how the other team is likely to handle screens. If you cannot execute a quick hitter successfully, the situation requires a precise approach because of the limited time. In selecting a play for this situation, consider assigning actual seconds to every pass and dribble to determine how much movement and activity players can afford before taking the shot. If you assume, for example, that a pass and a dribble each take 1 second, you can gauge how much time you have before you must shoot. If you have eight seconds, you can't afford more than two dribbles and two passes if you want any chance of an offensive rebound in the event of a miss. Whatever play you use, accounting precisely for remaining time is crucial.

If there are fewer than five seconds on the clock, your options obviously are limited. You cannot afford more than a single dribble off the inbounds pass, and while you might get away with one more pass for a catch-and-shoot off a screen, everything must go smoothly for that to work. Consider augmenting your playbook with a designed lob or a relatively quick catch-and-shoot-type play. There is not enough time to worry about trying to force a foul, other than hoping that a habitually ingrained up-fake draws contract. But specifically playing for the foul—which normally does not bring sympathy from officials—is risky.

Down Two, on the Foul Line with Two Shots to Take, and 10 Seconds or Less Remaining

You should have your best rebounders on the line, and all players should assume a miss. Here are the options:

1. If you make both shots and tie the game, and are put in an immediate defensive mode, do you call timeout or at least have a

substitute at the table (after the shooter gets the ball from the referee) to slow down the offense and set up your defense?

2. If you miss the first one, you are in the situation described in chapter 2, where you need to miss the second shot on purpose.

3. If you make the first and miss the second and don't get the offensive rebound, you must foul immediately.

Down One or Two, with the Ball, and Less Than 10 Seconds to Play, Inbounding the Ball under the Opposite Basket

The threshold question is whether to start your offense full court (or must if you lack a timeout) or get to halfcourt quickly, call a timeout, and discuss a halfcourt play. The former approach can work if you have an excellent ball handler with speed who can dribble the full length of the court and get to the basket strongly. Those with good memories (or who are fond of YouTube clips) will recall the coast-to-coast play by Danny Ainge of Brigham Young University against Notre Dame in the 1981 NCAA Tournament. Ainge got the ball under his own basket with eight seconds left, executed three crossover dribbles in open court as he navigated defenders like a deft master of Pac-Man, and scored the winning basket with a short runner in the lane with two seconds remaining. If you lack a Danny Ainge clone, you can use the timeout at halfcourt approach (see the opening scenario in chapter 13). A middle ground is to push the ball hard to see how it goes and, once at halfcourt, if you do not like what you see, call timeout. Of course, if you have no timeouts, you are, by default, looking to pull a Danny Ainge.

Down One or Two, with 10 Seconds or Less Left, with the Other Team on the Foul Line with One Shot

This is similar to the preceding situation. Regardless of the foul-shot result, you are in a one-possession game with limited time to get down the floor. You have three initial options: 1) call timeout after the foul shot, 2) get the rebound and try to make a quick play down the floor before the defense gets settled, or 3) get to halfcourt and call timeout. Your election may depend on the specific amount of time on the clock. And regardless of when you call timeout, you may want to address with the team more than the one possession.

Down Three, with the Ball, and Ample Time to Get off a Good Shot

This situation underscores—and can put in conflict—the probabilities of strategic options and coaching style. Needless to say, hitting a three to tie the game leaves you a stop away from a chance to win in overtime or, better yet, a chance to win in regulation if you can get a stop or turnover with ample time for one more successful possession. If you are bold, you might opt for this approach and call a play designed to free your best shooters. On the other hand, playing for a three-point shot is a gamble. If it does not work, you risk facing a two-possession game—either because you have to foul and put the other team on the foul line or, worse, suffer a long rebound off the perimeter shot and a transition basket—with even less time on the clock. Which situation is more probable? Which strategy suits your style? Are the answers the same?

A middle ground is to get a "quick two," or possibly three, points after a foul, by attacking the basket at the earliest opportunity. If you draw the foul, the clock stops, with a chance for three points. Attacking the basket might also allow you to get the ball off dribble penetration to a perimeter shooter with a good look for a high-percentage three.

If you attack the basket and get a score without a foul call, you can stop the action with a timeout. Keep in mind that getting two points rather than three is a good result. A quick two moves the game to a one-point margin, allows you to foul quickly after the make, and shifts the pressure to the other team. One missed foul shot means a two-point game and a significant change in the outcome percentages in your favor. Again, this is where practice is important. The team must be efficient in these moments.

Down Three, with the Ball, and Less Than 10 Seconds on the Clock

Here, there is little question that the preferred option is a three-point shot attempt. If you have to travel the full length of the court, you might sprint to halfcourt to call timeout. If you have the ball sideline out-of-bounds in your territory, you have a few seconds to play with. In either case, you need a well-designed and practiced play to free a shooter, with a backup option, since the other team likely will key on your best or hottest shooter.

Consider, too, that the other team might foul to prevent a three-point attempt, which is covered in chapter 2. How do you handle the anticipated foul, which will come quickly and maybe on the first catch? A quick catch-and-shoot play that uses one pass, perhaps coming off a screen, can allow enough separation to get a good look before the defense adjusts.

If the other coach prefers not to foul to take away the three-point shot and you cannot get a quick look from the perimeter or you lack a strong perimeter game, the other option is to attack the rim, looking for contact, a successful finish, and a trip to the foul line. If you only net two points, you have to foul with a few seconds left and see what that brings.

Down Four or More, with the Ball, with Sufficient Time to Run a Halfcourt Set

This situation suggests running an efficient halfcourt set for a high-percentage shot. While a three-point attempt can work, the odds favor a relatively quick score through a higher-percentage shot to make it a two-point game, as a missed three digs a deeper hole. In either case, if you don't score, you are in an immediate fouling mode. If you score, depending on time left on the clock, you can seek a turnover, but if you are not successful, you will have to foul pretty quickly.

The related question is whether to press, with its benefits and risks. Which is more probable: success off a press or success off fouling? Should you combine both approaches? If you conclude that fouling is inevitable, the earlier you start the process, the better your chances of success, especially if you are able to trade two points for one each time. Sure, a turnover can be huge, but the probability of causing one should be weighed against diminishing time on the clock and how well the other team tends to value the ball. A well-executed fouling strategy can be the best bet to pull a rabbit out of the hat. Play the perceived probabilities.

Defense

Down Two and Defending, with Sufficient Time for the Other Team to Run a Halfcourt Set

Coaching style differs here. Some play for a turnover before starting to foul. Others foul quickly to maximize time for the next possession. Both have advantages and disadvantages. If you can get the turnover, you have a chance for the last shot and a tie or win. Playing for the turnover, however, risks running valuable time off the clock. A quick foul freezes time and extends the game with the countervailing risk of giving up one or two points, the latter creating a two-possession game. Decision factors include the level of skill of your pressure or trapping defense, the decision-making ability of your players, and the foul-shooting ability of the other team. Unless and until the game is tied, *time* is the biggest hurdle to overcome. Thus, the odds favor an early foul.

Down 3, and Defending, with 10 Seconds Left, and the Offense Has the Ball at the Other End of the Floor

Options are limited. You need the ball. Every second deepens the final nail in the coffin. You can double-team the likely receiver and try to force a five-second call or try to steal the inbounds pass. But if either fails, you have to foul immediately.

Down Four or More, and Defending the Final Possession

The odds, in a two-possession game with the shot clock off, call for an immediate foul.

LAST-POSSESSION SITUATIONS WHEN AHEAD

Offense

When ahead with the ball in a last-possession situation, the twin goals are simple: value the ball and burn clock. While the other team likely will start to foul, yours should know how to play "keep-away." Players too often accept the foul readily, taking away opportunities to keep the clock ticking via ball movement. While you can't keep the ball away forever, a well-practiced drill for this purpose advances the cause.

In addition, and a recurring theme, have your best foul shooters on the floor. If you prefer to go with a particular player or two for defensive purposes, for example, rim protection, whose foul shooting leaves something to be desired, your keep-away drill should keep the ball away from that player as well. Alternatively, you can use offense-to-defense substitutions (see chapter 3) to try to keep poor foul shooters off the floor.

Your team must be sensitized to defenders hunting passing lanes in this situation. Players must be reminded that a defender is lurking about looking to steal their next pass. They should get vision on the culprit and either pull them out of position with the invaluable pass fake or move the ball elsewhere. And pass receivers should know to come to the ball.

Again, do you have a rule for when, if ever, it is acceptable to shoot in this situation? As with other situations, consider a mandate that the only acceptable shot is an uncontested layup.

Also consider preparing for specific situations. For instance, assume you are up one or two with less than 10 seconds left and inbounding the ball under the opponent's basket. Do you have an inbounds set that gets the ball on the first pass to your best free-throw shooter with a counter should the other team deny that pass or not guard the inbounds passer and double-team your best free-throw shooter?

If your possession came off a make and you have to bring the ball full court for the last possession, anticipate pressure. Make sure players know they can run baseline on the inbounds pass after a made basket, which a floor leader should confirm with an official. And, again, consider a timeout to settle the team down and remind them to take their time, stay poised, use pass fakes, and find defenders lying in wait for the steal. Remind them of the details of your press break and any keep-away set you want them to implement, and so on.

Defense

If you are defending the final possession when ahead, the strategy is simple: Do not foul, get a stop, and win. Before discussing discrete situations, here are several general considerations.

First, and paramount, if possible before the change of possession, do you call a timeout to plan the defensive possession? Alternatively, as discussed in chapter 1, have your assistant on the lookout to see if the other team is about to call a timeout and gift you a "free" one. If not, seriously consider calling your own. The last image you want to see before you go to sleep the night of the game is watching the other team quickly inbound the ball and sprint the length of the floor for a high-percentage shot and the win, as recounted in the opening scenario. If you are inclined to call the timeout, alert the referees it is coming "on the make." True, the countervailing factor is the offense gets to set up too. But the stop probabilities increase when you can set up your defense, refocus the team, and review the precious small things. Players need reminders.

Second, do you play your best defensive five or at least the best defensive five for the offensive plan you are likely to see? And, of course, do not forget the option of "offense-to-defense" substitution, as discussed in chapter 3.

Third, do you want your players to take a charge as they might in the normal course of a game or avoid charge attempts because of the risk of a block call?

Fourth, do you consider playing zone to confuse the other team, slow them down, and make dribble penetration more difficult? Or do you get bold and trap a ball handler or pass receiver, or double-team the post?

Fifth, do you try to force the opposing best player to give up the ball and force another player to try to beat you?

Sixth, if you get the stop, and thus expect the other team to foul immediately, does your team know to get the ball into the hands of your best foul shooter?

The following are some specific situations when defending at the end.

Up Two, and Defending, with Sufficient Time for the Other Team to Run a Halfcourt Set

The threshold question here is whether to pick up full court or halfcourt. The former, if executed well—avoiding risks of fouling and getting beat off the dribble—robs the other team of precious seconds for their preferred offensive set and possibly changes the spot on the floor where they prefer to initiate. When you pick up at halfcourt or full court, be clear on how you want your players to defend.

- Do they switch all screens or only ball screens, fight over screens, hedge, or do something else entirely?
- Should they force the ball sideline and baseline or into interior help?

- Do wing defenders help on a penetration or show only and stay home with shooters?
- Do all five hit the defensive glass on a shot?
- Do you double-team the post on ball entry?
- Do you trap the ball in specific spots, like the wings or short corners?
- Do you play zone and bottle up penetration, and risk the outside shot?
- And, again, as stressed in the prior chapter, do you allow the other team to easily roll the ball up the floor on the inbounds "pass" to delay start of the clock?

Up One or Two, and Defending, with about Five Seconds or Less Left, and the Other Team Must Go the Length of the Floor

Here, the offense is looking for a desperation play—either a baseball pass and catch-and-shoot, or a two, or a few long dribbles and a shot. The threshold question is, Do you guard the inbounds passer or double-team the likely intended inbounds pass receiver? This calls to mind one of the most thrilling moments in NCAA basketball history, in the 1992 East Regional final between Kentucky and Duke in the Meadowlands. With 2.1 seconds left in overtime, Duke, down one, had the ball under the Kentucky basket. Duke looked done. Kentucky, however, decided not to guard the inbounds pass (for various reasons), and Grant Hill of Duke threw an unobstructed pass three-quarters of the way down the floor and into the waiting arms of Christian Laettner (who had not missed a shot all game). Laettner caught the ball cleanly and, after misdirection, made a turnaround jumper at the buzzer for the win.

To contest the inbounds pass in that situation, it helps to have a player of size experienced enough to avoid an interference call or a charge if the inbounder runs the baseline. Kentucky felt it had neither, with two of their experienced bigs fouled out. In all events, the probabilities commend defending the inbounds pass. Make things difficult for the other team. Obstructing the vision of the passer is important, as it would be in the halfcourt in this situation as well. The other team needs near-perfect execution to win. The more obstacles you deposit in their path, the lower the odds of their success.

Moreover, most teams who must travel full court with only several seconds in a game want the ball in the hands of their most creative and reliable player, someone who can make plays under stress as the buzzer looms. Why let that player have the ball? Why not make someone else try to be the hero? Whether you double-team them on the inbounds pass or try to deny them the pass, consider action specifically to keep the ball out of their hands.

A case in point was the 2016 NCAA Championship final between Villanova and North Carolina. After UNC's Marcus Paige capped an extraordinary UNC comeback with an acrobatic three to tie the game with 4.7 seconds remaining, Villanova called timeout, giving both teams the opportunity to plan those precious seconds. After the timeout, Villanova playmaker and floor leader Ryan Arcidiacono received the inbounds pass from under the UNC basket without being contested. On the catch, in one-on-one coverage, Arcidiacono dribbled three-quarters of the way down the floor, drew defenders, and dished to and gave a brush screen for the trailing Kris Jenkins, who hit the game-winning shot in stride at the buzzer. Second-guessing is convenient, but you have to wonder why Arcidiacono had that kind of freedom in that kind of moment.

Up Two, and Defending, with Seven Seconds Left, and the Other Team Has the Ball Sideline Out of Bounds

This situation requires a precise strategy. Most teams try to get the ball either to the player who can best create off the dribble or shoot well off the catch. If you feel you know the likely pass receiver, do you deny them the ball, and if they manage to get the catch, double-team them on the catch? If you double-team before the ball is inbounded and don't guard the inbounds passer, know if the inbounds passer is a good shooter. The initial pass receiver might reverse the ball to the entry passer for a quick shot. Or do you deny all potential receivers and play straight-up defense on the catch? This is another situation where switching everything can be effective. In any event, be specific about how defenders are to handle screens. Whatever you do, be prepared for all probabilities. Losing in this situation is a tough pill to swallow.

Up Three, and Defending, with Sufficient (but Barely Enough) Time for a Three-Point Attempt

This situation is covered extensively in chapter 2. It recurs often enough to warrant practice time.

Up Three, and Defending, with Ample Time for the Other Team to Get Off a Good Shot

Unlike the previous situation, it is risky to foul early to take away an attempted three-point shot. Fouling, first and foremost, stops the clock, which aids the opposition. It also risks putting you in a one-point or, if on a three-point attempt, tie game with ample time for bad things to happen. An important question is whether to prepare for the three-point shot by stacking defenders above the arc, like in a 3–2 zone, or play in-the-grill man defense above the perimeter that risks dribble penetration into interior help defense. The challenge for players is to avoid giving referees reasons to blow whistles, especially in favor of a shooter, a risk for which players need repeated reminders. The exception is effective dribble penetration. If someone gets beat on an attack to the basket, help defenders should know not to allow a clean shot and, if necessary, to foul hard to prevent a bucket or even a clean attempt. Make them earn two points from the line. You might get lucky and limit them to one or no points (see chapter 2).

※ ※ ※

Last possessions in close games are flush with options. The more teams practice them with variables and the more coaches break them down and review them during practice, the more likely teams will be to execute successfully when facing these exciting competitive moments.

9

GAME MATCHUPS

"It's tough to make predictions, especially about the future."—Yogi
Berra

The next team we face features a guard who literally is a one-man
show. Often scoring more than 60 percent of his team's points, he
does it all: hits midrange and perimeter jumpers (from way beyond
the arc); leads the break with force and attacks the basket hard off
the dribble, often drawing contact; feeds off the foul line; and swal-
lows rebounds. The next year, as a senior, he will be one of the
leading high school scorers in the nation. He is more than two hand-
fuls.

We have a choice: play our normal defense and assume one
player cannot beat us, a reasonable approach since on paper we are
unquestionably the better team, or employ something special to try
to control him. I am anxious about the prospects of a player putting
40 or more on us and carrying the day. This anxiety tips the balance
in favor of special treatment. We decide to use a platoon defense that
shows him different defensive styles and keeps our guys out of foul
trouble. We will double- and sometimes triple-team him to force him
to give up the ball and see if his teammates can step up. We will have
whomever he guards attack the basket as often as practical to draw
fouls and see if we can make him a spectator. Our defensive plan, for
intents and purposes, is one-man centric.

It works. We deny him most clean outside looks and force him to
seek points going to the cup. Every time he puts the ball on the floor,
we send a posse at him. He gets to the line often enough, but he also

gets frustrated, leading to some bad decisions. His teammates begin to stand around and lose focus. We hold him to under his substantial average and win by more than 20.

No check-the-box list exists for determining defensive assignments. The baseline of matching up by position and size can be simplistic. Various other considerations can shape a sound matchup strategy. Here are some to think about.

First, matchup strategy begins with an honest critique of personnel, including habits, decision-making tendencies, egos, competitiveness, toughness, and how well a player handles specific assignments. These factors inform both initial assignments and matchup adjustments.

Second, if the other team has a dominant offensive guard or small forward, the logical choice is your best on-the-ball defender, especially if limiting this player is a key to victory. Ideally, the defender should also be adept at off-the-ball defense, since ball denial and deft navigation of screens are important when covering a dominant player. A countervailing consideration arises if your preferred assignment happens to be *your* key offensive player. If they pile up some fouls, the assignment may be a shot in the foot. A related concern is fatigue. If your best offensive player exerts substantial energy at the defensive end, they may have little left in the tank on offense down the stretch. As a safeguard, when dealing with a dominant player, consider a platoon system to minimize both risks.

Third, if the other team has a big who can give you fits, especially in the low-post area, apart from a double-team strategy (see later in this chapter), the natural assignment is your best-defending big, unless, again, foul-trouble considerations favor another player.

Fourth, if your game strategy includes defensive help on a specific matchup, consider assigning the help defender to the other team's weakest offensive player. That allows the help defender to hedge strong, double-team, or trap, assuming the perceived defensive advantage outweighs risks associated with leaving the assigned player open.

Fifth, do any assignments risk putting any of your players in foul trouble? The answer might influence initial assignment or substitution decisions (see also chapter 3).

Sixth, does rebounding figure prominently in the upcoming game, especially if you face a team that produces second-chance opportunities? If so, consider a rebound-oriented assignment; for example, matching your best defensive rebounder with their best offensive rebounder.

Seventh, if the other team leaks players for transition advantage or otherwise relies heavily on transition, assign specific positions to handle defensive balance. For example, you can have the guard on the perimeter be responsible for getting back on defense on the shot. If both guards are up top, both can retreat on the shot.

Eighth, it is fundamental, and crucial, to have a matchup plan for ball screens, especially when teams use them to free up their best offensive threat. Do you switch the screens (and risk matchup problems), try to go over them (and risk getting beat), double-team the ball off the screen, and dare someone else to hurt you or go under the screen, especially when the offensive threat is more a driver than a perimeter shooter?

Ninth, there is the creative realm, an assignment that defies coaching logic and custom. Consider the defensive adjustment of the Golden State Warriors in the 2015 NBA Conference Semifinals against the Memphis Grizzlies. To offset the inside advantages of Memphis in the persons of Marc Gasol and Zach Randolph, the Warriors moved center Andrew Bogut off Gasol and onto Tony Allen, a relatively poor shooting guard. This unconventional assignment allowed Bogut to cheat off Allen and help inside against Gasol and Randolph. While this often left Allen open, the Warriors gambled that Allen could not capitalize, at least not enough to outweigh the benefits from the inside help. The strategy worked brilliantly.

SMALL BALL

Finally, matchup strategy can be team-wide, like the "small-ball" lineup, which is increasingly popular. Small ball typically sacrifices size, strength, low-post offense, and interior defense in favor of speed, quickness, shooting ability, increased scoring potential, and enhanced perimeter and on-the ball defense. While it can take various forms, a small-ball unit typically comprises three guards and two forwards. A variation is five guards to enhance scoring and increase tempo.

On the other hand, small ball can compromise rim protection and expose the team to superior post-up play. Rebounding also can be sacrificed. If a team goes small, coaches must remind players how to exploit the advantages and minimize the disadvantages. For example,

- Increase energy when defending on the ball and hunting passing lanes.
- Isolate pick-and-roll combinations to create favorable matchups.
- Isolate one-on-one opportunities to allow a good shooting "small" to take a "big" defender off the dribble and create off penetration.
- Dominate the 50–50 game: Make loose balls and rebounding a major priority (and heed the inviolate assumption that every shot is a potential miss).
- Push the ball: Playing uptempo can wear down the opposition, especially if they are uncomfortable playing baseline to baseline and prefer the haven of halfcourt.
- Space the floor widely, keep the ball and defenders moving, and attack the paint.

✿ ✿ ✿

Matchup musings may be the most intriguing pregame discussions among a coaching staff. Because they attempt to predict how players will respond to anticipated challenges, they often have no set-in-stone answers. At bottom, matchup-probability analysis springs from judgment informed by knowledge of players on both teams. The safety net is that game assignments can be changed if initial predictions are off.

10

MANAGING THE BLOWOUT GAME

"Everybody pulls for David, nobody roots for Goliath."—Wilt Chamberlain

I am coaching a talented girls' varsity high school team, easily 40 points better than many teams we face. Offensively, we are uptempo, and defensively, we full-court press and trap in the halfcourt. We will finish 27–3, losing our last game to the eventual state champs, with a number-five ranking in our California state division.

As the season unfolds, we receive criticism about our win margins. Despite what the critics seem to think, I am sensitive to how we impact other teams. I also, however, want to maximize success for my team in what looms a special year for our basketball program. I consult my brother John, a former Division I college coach who has moved on to the professional level, and we develop a list of adjustments for blowout games that will allow my team to stay sharp and competitive, while easing up on other teams. The changes, however, hardly enthuse my players. In one imbalanced game, our leading scorer, who would go on to play at a Division I school, says, "Coach, I can't get up for these kids."

Still, criticism continues, including from the media. So, in our final league game against a school we beat by more than 50 points earlier in the season, I experiment to show there is a limit to what we can and should do in these situations. Before the tip, I inform the other coach we will 1) not press, 2) not play man defense (but a nontrapping halfcourt 1–2–2 zone), 3) sit our starters more than normal (notwithstanding a college scout in the stands), and 4) pull off the fast break early.

Despite these major changes, the final score is 61–20. The opposing coach candidly acknowledges that our substantial adjustments did little for his girls and were a severe disservice to my players, who, as he metaphorically puts it, "had the wind taken out of them."

If you coach this great game long enough, you will find yourself on both sides of the blowout contest, and likely more than once. Everyone, from coaches, parents, and administrators to the media, has an opinion about how to manage blowout games, particularly at the high school level. Other than legislated "mercy rules"—which typically impose a running clock when the score margin reaches a certain point, for example, 40 points—the lopsided game is not regulated. Indeed, many oppose such rules, arguing, among other things, that they do more harm than good, are patronizing, even if well-intentioned, and improperly intrude upon coaching judgment and discretion. Coaches who resist compelled adjustments might find comfort in the words of Bill Shakespeare: "The quality of mercy is not strained."

Lopsided games also trigger concerns about sportsmanship and how best to serve the impacted athletes. The criticisms of teams charged with running up scores distill to how, at certain game intervals, they continue to use 1) pressure defenses (whether full-court presses or halfcourt traps), 2) transition offense, 3) three-point shooting, 4) starting players, and 5) a dominant player piling up stats.

Managing the lopsided contest is not as easy as the casual observer may presume. To be sure, coaches can make game adjustments to reduce the impact of an overwhelming loss on the other team. Coaches are, however, also duty-bound to do what is best for their team and its players, and, I submit, are uniquely situated to determine how to do so. While some coaches are constitutionally unable or flat-out unwilling to take their foot off the accelerator, others believe a line exists that teams with massive leads should not cross. But agreement on where to draw the line is less clear. Before getting into specifics of each side of the blowout experience, consider two threshold dynamics.

First, when substantially ahead, how do you determine a comeback is beyond reasonable possibility? In some situations, it can be before the game starts, when there is no question the two teams operate on completely different playing levels. In other situations, it might not occur until sometime in the second half. Second, the lopsided game can impede the progress and damper the motivation of the superior team.

What is the fair balance between what to do and when to do it? The interplay produces grey areas different coaches doubtless will handle differently. Is it fair, for example, to ask bench players to play a different style than emphasized in practice? Is it fair to leave "star" players on the floor in the fourth quarter to allow second-rotation players a chance to play competitively with them? Is it crossing the line for a coach to play a star player deep into the final period of a high school blowout when college coaches are scouting?

In the end, how to handle a blowout game ultimately is a coaching judgment call that weighs and balances short-term and long-term team goals, personnel, game circumstances, and program values. I believe space exists for inspired changes to manage the lopsided game in a manner that serves both teams well. Dialogue about the management of blowout games can produce a more balanced understanding of the considerations and more creative solutions. The following are some considerations from both sides of the scorer's table.

THE WINNING SIDE OF THE BLOWOUT

The blowout game can be rich with opportunities to enhance team and individual skills that otherwise might not get sufficient or any attention in a competitive contest. Once it becomes clear that a comeback is not possible, coaches can make adjustments that foster improvement in areas where the team needs work without compromising team goals and indeed advancing them, while easing up on the other team. Here are some examples:

- Take off the transition game in favor of concentrating on halfcourt offense. Impose a minimum pass requirement to stress patience, excellent passing, sound decision making, and good shot selection. Teams cannot get enough work on their halfcourt offenses, and these games provide a bountiful opportunity to improve in that area.

- Make adjustments at both ends that help your players improve and at the same time help the other team gain some game traction. For instance, put a big on one of their small forwards or guards to give your player an opportunity to work on defensive fundamentals, especially footwork, while giving the opposing player the chance to create off the dribble.
- Remove full-court pressure and concentrate on halfcourt defense by, for example, picking up dribblers after they cross halfcourt, playing tough on-the-ball defense, and denying passes to the wings. Have your team concentrate on getting deflections, and identify a team deflection goal. Such adjustments maintain defensive intensity and focus, and can pay dividends down the road, especially during postleague competition, while giving the other team more breathing room to progress.
- Challenge your players to step outside their comfort zone. For instance, have ball handlers attack the basket with their "weak" hand. Ask a post player to execute a low-post move you have been after them to master. Have a big bring the ball up to work on their handles. Ask players who need work on setting screens to set them each time down the floor.
- The most obvious perhaps is to limit the minutes of starters. The blowout game is the ideal time to share opportunities to contribute. You might consider making substitutions in stages to ease the sting of humiliation from wholesale changes. It is important, too, to be positive about the minutes these games provide other players. Opportunities to play in a blowout game are still opportunities to play.
- Consider a rule that at some point players take only layups, an important discipline for other game situations.
- Here is perhaps a not-so-obvious thought: Ask the other coach what is best for their team, like what occurs in preseason scrimmages. While you may get asked to do something you prefer not to do, the interaction will inspire deeper understanding, enhance sportsmanship and coaching camaraderie, and might generate adjustments that serve both teams.

No doubt, other examples exist to maintain the edge you want for your team, while diffusing the impact of the onslaught. Creativity in this situation is boundless.

THE LOSING SIDE OF THE BLOWOUT

Despite the understandable instinct to hope for a turnaround, at some point coaches must be realistic and focus on ways to teach and learn from the lopsided situation. A coach should not bang their head against the proverbial wall looking for ways to win when winning indisputably is not an option. And worrying about the precise margin of loss in these situations—a superficial consideration—misses the chance to realize the prospects of long-term benefits. Competing and learning are always options. It also an ideal circumstance for everyone involved to learn how to handle adversity. While admittedly a challenge, getting players to keep their heads up and spirits alive in a blowout is nonetheless an important goal.

Athletes tend to be resilient, and coaches tend to understand the value of the big picture and long-term goals. If a team, for example, has not developed skills in dealing with full-court pressure or a trapping defense, should they welcome the opportunity to work against those defenses? How will they otherwise improve? Putting aside emotional angst and frustration, the blowout game provides ample teaching and learning opportunities.

- Identify new team goals. For instance, set specific defensive goals (e.g., a consecutive number of stops) and redefine goals for the offense (e.g., scoring at the rim after a set number of passes). Send five to the glass, even at the risk of transition—again, at some point the scoreboard is irrelevant—to develop a second-chance rebounding mentality.
- Motivate players with different opportunities. Give the ball to that off-guard who wants time at the point. Let guards post up if practical. Think outside the box to identify ways to build confidence and develop skills, and make adjustments to keep players "in the game."

- Be more communicative than normal. Be positive about specific performance, whether it is mere effort or a good pass or rebound. A coach can revive the spirit that blowouts can otherwise dampen and improve coaching skills in the process. Set an example for behavior. Make your players proud to be part of the team, and make character development an overriding accomplishment in this situation. They have two choices: mope and hang their heads or redouble their efforts, push past any embarrassment, exude enthusiasm, and take pride in themselves.
- Postgame behavior is important here too. Inspire your players to keep their heads up and display sportsmanship.

✿ ✿ ✿

Blowouts are an indelible part of the athletic mosaic. They can be handled with class, creativity, intelligence, and compassion. Approached from a constructive and balanced perspective, they challenge coaches to manage games and present opportunities from which teams on either side of the aisle can extract long-term benefits not generally available in competitive contests. Regardless of which side of the blowout game teams are on, players and coaches should be respectful, show sportsmanship, honor the game, and work hard to improve skills and team performance.

11

THE JUMP BALL

"I play in the over-40 basketball league. We don't have jump balls. The ref just puts the ball on the floor, and whoever can bend over and pick it up gets possession."—Anonymous

In my high school coaching world, players taller than 6-foot-6 are uncommon. We now face a team with a 6-foot-8 center, and watching various films, we note they habitually get an easy bucket off the jump ball. Their center tips the ball to the power forward at the center of the circle, who, in turn, passes to one of their two guards storming to the basket on the tip, typically creating a 2-on-1 situation.

I want to concede neither the possession nor the make. It seems we have little to lose trying to undermine their time-tested ritual at the opening tip. We practice a counter where, on the tip, we send the two players who match up with their leaking guards at the intended receiver, one to face-guard and seal him, and the other to glide into the passing lane to try to get a hand on the ball. Timing is crucial; otherwise, we risk a lane violation. We do not care whether we score off the jump; we want to deny them the possession and an early basket and shake things up a little.

I am excited to try this. Amazingly, we steal the tip and, better yet, because the steal puts the other team out of sorts (and position), we convert the steal. Armed with newfound enthusiasm, we get two consecutive stops and score on our next two possessions, staking a 6–0 lead. The early momentum is a major boost; we have to overachieve against this much stronger team. We sustain the initial ener-

gy and take the game to the wire, losing on two foul shots in the last
10 seconds. That we came within one possession of a major upset is
in part attributable to the momentum and confidence we garnered
from the jump-ball strategy. Concede nothing.

The center jump occurs, without exception, each game, at the same
time, and in the same game conditions. It is a possession moment and
no less a "little thing" than the litany of little things we ask players to
execute in games. Coaches generally agree that every possession is important, and while some are more important than others, we hate wasting even a single one. Why should the center jump "possession" be any
different?

The center jump tends to get little attention because coaches are 1)
resigned to losing the possession, 2) content to win the jump and comfortably run their halfcourt offense, or 3) uncertain who will win the
jump and elect to play it conservatively. There are, however, different
perspectives to consider.

In the first scenario, when your team likely will be outjumped, the
choice is either to accept your fate and retreat quickly to play halfcourt
defense or try to steal the possession and possibly score. The former is
safe and relatively risk free. The latter flows from a philosophy that
seeks to maximize the number of possessions in each game.

In the second scenario, where you are confident you will win the tip,
the two options are equally clear: get the possession and comfortably set
up your halfcourt offense or aggressively seek an early offense opportunity.

The third scenario is a combination of the first two.

While a more aggressive approach may not always work, it sometimes will and can be exploited with little risk, if practiced enough.
Teams generally are lax in the jump-ball moment, and the element of
surprise can create early game excitement and momentum.

Consider having at least two and possibly three options available and
practiced (especially in intrasquad scrimmages): 1) an attack looking for
early offense; 2) stealing the tip; and, possibly, 3) committing a jump-
ball violation to foil an expected easy basket for the other team.

WHEN LIKELY TO LOSE THE TIP

When you are likely to lose the tip, the first thing to consider is where the opposing center likes to tip the ball, which can be unearthed through scouting. If known, as soon as the ball goes up, send a player into the favored passing lane and seek the steal. If you do not know where the ball is likely to go, there are three likely tipping options: 1) behind the jumper to the player positioned for defensive balance, usually near the top of the key; 2) directly in front of the jumper to a fellow post player on the strong side; or 3) to the wing on the side where the center jumper is facing. On the toss, send the designated players into these three passing lanes. One will have a reasonable chance of pay dirt. This leaves open the player on the wing, who is the least likely to get the ball because, to do so, the jumper must tip awkwardly in the opposite direction they are facing. And, even there, the risk is not great since you have your fifth player back for defensive balance. Know that in the chaos that might follow, the initial game matchups might not hold up, and players must know to communicate defensive coverages out of the tip if the ball is not stolen. Again, regular practice will help players adjust in the moment.

WHEN LIKELY TO WIN THE TIP

Where likely to win the tip, consider having two plays available. In both cases, have someone back for defensive balance. The other four figure directly in the execution of the play. There are many plays to use in this situation. An illustration can be found in the opening scenario.

WHEN LIKELY TO SUFFER A MAKE OFF THE TIP

Finally, there is the situation—which seldom occurs—where because of the size, strength, and style of the other team, the odds are your team will suffer a make off the tip and, for whatever reason, you are not confident you can steal the tip. One solution: Violate the jump. That way, while you concede the possession, you eliminate the fast-break play off the tip and force the other team to initiate their offense out of bounds, allowing your team to set up its halfcourt defense. If you elect this course, your team captain may want to alert officials to the impending violation so they don't miss the call. There are several ways to trigger the violation. The two easiest are 1) the player handling the jump exits the circle as soon as the official throws the ball up (and *before* the ball is tipped), or 2) another player enters the circle *before* the ball is tipped.

❂ ❂ ❂

Coaches can view the opening tip in one of two ways: a necessary ritual or an early opportunity. If you are confident you can manage the risks, why not try to exploit the opportunity? At a minimum, exploring this in practice to see how players handle what you devise seems a small investment for the potential (recurring) payoff.

12

OVERTIME

"I've never lost a game. I just ran out of time."—Michael Jordan

Short four players because of injuries and illness, and at a severe disadvantage before we take the floor, we quickly find ourselves in a possession-by-possession battle and war of attrition. Worse, the referees apparently are in hot pursuit of a new record for most whistles blown in a single game in the shot clock era, an ambition that sends two of my players to the bench, disqualified with maximum fouls. We are at risk of finishing the game with less than five available players.

We have the ball in a tie game with 16 seconds left, which should give us the final possession unless we shoot too early. Even though we are down to six players and I worry that a full squad might not survive an OT, I still see overtime as an important option. I call timeout and tell the team I don't care if we don't get a shot off: The only option is a high-percentage shot near or at the buzzer. Under no circumstances can we give the other team any time on the clock. Either we win on this possession with no time left or take our chances in OT with our decimated corps. We get the last shot and miss as time runs out.

We have gotten this far with a tenacious man defense that deployed halfcourt traps, a counterintuitive move in the circumstances that naturally took its toll on my guys. The other team did not adjust well, and, in theory at least, the trapping should be our ticket in the OT. But my guys understandably are gassed, with two of my surviving six in foul trouble. If we stay with what got us here, I fear we will literally fall flat on our faces. I discard the aggressive defense and opt to play zone. The adjustment works. We get an early lead, the other team can't solve the zone, and we control the pace during the OT and net the W.

Is overtime merely an extension of the game, a four- or five-minute mini-me of regulation? Whatever worked in regulation should work again in overtime, correct? Or is overtime unique and qualitatively different than regulation?

Well, for starters, overtime *feels* different. It is more stressful. Players are more eager. Coaches are tenser. Fans, whose anxiety normally is abnormal, in overtime tend to succumb to a manic pitch. A sense of urgency envelopes the gym. Each moment is felt. Overtimes are cut from a different cloth, and they etch in the collective memory deeper than most other games.

There are other considerations. How did you get to overtime? Was it a back-and-forth game for an extended period or most or all of the game? Did one team stage a heroic comeback to tie the game near or at the end? If the latter, how will your team likely react in the overtime to the surge they experienced in regulation, regardless of which side of that dynamic they are on? What impact, if any, can you assume from whether you are playing at home or away? Knowing the internal make-up of your players is ever so important here.

THE CONDITION OF PLAYERS AT OVERTIME

The most important coaching challenge in overtime may be managing the spirit and emotional condition of players. There also is physical fatigue to take into account. In overtime, players must draw a little extra from their internal reservoir of energy to close out the overtime period (and maybe another). How much energy did your team expend getting the game into overtime or trying to prevent overtime? Which players have the greatest staying power beyond regulation? Which players are on the cusp of exhaustion? In constructing a strategic approach to overtime, consider the state of being of your athletes.

MENTAL TOUGHNESS CONSIDERATIONS

Overtime is ripe for pressing players into service who are most up to the task of performing under pressure. Overtime can quickly get away from a team that endures a couple of early bad possessions. The team that executes with poise and patience, and demonstrates the best take-charge ability, will have the edge in the extra frame. More than ever, shot selection, second-chance opportunities, and smart individual and team defense crammed into a four- or five-minute package are the ingredients for overtime success. Equally important, as in the comeback situation, is turnover control. Overtime mistakes are magnified because of limited time and the stress of the situation. Urge your team to have greater patience and value the ball on each possession.

POSSESSION MANAGEMENT

Keep in mind too that unlike regulation periods, you have fewer possessions in overtime. Using the baseline of 23 seconds per possession, a five-minute overtime produces seven possessions per team, a number that will decrease rapidly. Overtime possessions arguably are more valuable than regulation possession, especially if you assume the first few can set a tone that can demoralize the other team and carry the day. How do you use this wasting asset? Does your overtime strategy include consideration of the limited available possessions? Do you want to increase pressure and try to wreak havoc to get an early psychological edge?

Also recall that overtime begins with a jump ball (see chapter 11). This is an opportunity, especially if you did not use one of your jump-ball plays at the start of the game or have a second one in the bank, to jump-start the overtime with a surprise. You will have under your belt the experience of the opening tip. Perhaps you learned something to yield advantage for the overtime jump ball.

FOUL SITUATION

Who is in foul trouble on both teams? How does the answer impact strategy, including substitutions? Does it suggest changing the defense, for example, shifting from man to a zone? Should you reconfigure matchups? Are there favorable matchups that did not exist in regulation that are now present because of foul trouble? Can you take more or fewer risks because of team fouls?

CHANGING DEFENSES

Depending on the circumstances, overtime can be an opportune time to spring a different defensive look. If your team is anxious or stressed, it is likely the other team is as well. Does it make sense, for example, to trot out a matchup or trapping zone to start the overtime to inject surprise and confusion? Again, a couple of early bad possessions for the other team may be all you need to grab control of the overtime.

TIMEOUTS

Timeouts in OT are as prized as ever. As time passes, and tension mounts, you must plan well for the overtime stretch run. Because management of the game is not business as usual in overtime, use of timeouts is crucial in this situation. Player and team intangibles are amplified, and coaches must monitor how overtime is playing out. You likely will need at least one timeout down the stretch and possibly more.

❄ ❄ ❄

Even if inclined to treat overtime like a tied game with five minutes left in the second half, you are still well served to take a deep breath, step away from the fray, and take general stock. Perhaps you will make no changes. But at least you will have taken an unobstructed view from outside the storm to formulate a thoughtful approach for the overtime period.

13

OUT-OF-BOUNDS SITUATIONS (SLOB AND BLOB)

"There are really only two plays, *Romeo and Juliet*, and put the darn ball in the basket."—Abe Lemons

In 2006, defending Division V California state champion Branson faced Modesto Christian for the second consecutive year in the semi-final game preceding the state championship. Branson won the prior year in OT against what most thought a superior team. The 2006 Modesto Christian team was even better, featuring four future NCAA Division I players.

Using an effective press, Modesto Christian held a steady lead throughout and led by six with two minutes to go. Branson, however, using its signature patience, clawed back. Down three with less than a minute left to play, Branson got a steal and converted. On the next possession, Branson fouled Modesto star Adrian Oliver in the act. Oliver missed both free throws, and Branson rebounded and brought the ball across halfcourt, where Branson head coach Jonas Honick called timeout. Eight seconds remained, and Branson, down one, had the ball on the sideline.

Branson players implicitly knew what to run. In a prior league game, they had executed an oft-practiced sideline out-of-bounds (SLOB) play that Honick had lifted from the San Antonio Spurs. Point guard Oliver McNally inbounded the ball, stepped onto the court, and paused as the ball reversed to three-point shooting threat David Liss for a presumed catch-and-shoot. Then McNally executed a flex cut toward the basket off staggered screens. Modesto Christian failed to communicate a screen switch, gifting McNally an unimpeded path to the basket. Liss beelined a pass to McNally, who made an uncontested layup, giving Branson a 53–52 lead. After the make, Modesto Christian heaved one that covered three-quarters of the court and grazed iron. Branson had earned another trip to the state championship, which they won. About the game-winning SLOB, McNally said, "I was confident coming out of the huddle because we've worked on it so much."

FROM THE OFFENSIVE PERSPECTIVE

SLOB and baseline out-of-bounds (BLOB) plays have multiple purposes. For that reason, coaches commonly include a variety of them in their playbook. As with halfcourt plays and defensive systems, voluminous materials exist in the public domain that describe more SLOB and BLOB plays than a coach will ever need or care to consider in a coaching career. The focus here is to help coaches select plays best suited for their programs and to stress, again, that these are valuable possessions.

SLOB and BLOB plays advance three main purposes:

1. To *score* 1) with a quick hitter at the rim, 2) off a set with multiple scoring options, and 3) via a quick-hitting three.
2. To *safely inbound* the ball and set up a halfcourt offense during the normal course of the game.
3. To *effectively inbound* the ball to a reliable foul shooter when the other team is seeking to foul to stop the clock and extend the game (see chapter 8).

The first option—to seek to score—reflects a philosophy to exploit all scoring opportunities. To succeed, players should be trained to execute with precision. Everyone must know who is responsible, coach or player, for calling the specific play. The assigned inbounder(s) should have good judgment and excellent passing skills. The other four should know instinctively to secure their assigned positions on the floor before the defense comfortably sets up. Moreover, have at least one inbounds play that works against both man and zone defenses.

The second situation—to inbound the ball safely—is self-explanatory, requiring basic screen work to free intended entry pass receivers. Players must be vigilant to watch for defenders hunting passing lanes, no matter what the situation. An inbounds entry pass is no casual event. Just ask Isaiah Thomas, whose casual pass against the Boston Celtics in the 1987 Eastern Conference Finals, snared by Larry Bird while hunting the passing lane, cost the Detroit Pistons a playoff game and, for all intents and purposes, a trip to the NBA Finals.

The third situation—inbounding the ball to a reliable foul shooter with a second option if the former is denied the ball—is covered in chapter 8.

In addition, do you have a separate play for the short-corner BLOB situation? While it does not occur regularly, it does happen, and it is different than the typical BLOB. The defense has an advantage because ball location in relation to the basket makes it difficult to get the ball directly to the weak side. Screens are ever-important here, as is misdirection, since you want to take advantage of the strong-side overload and the tendency to overplay in that direction.

Finally, have a rule for when your players should break into their movements on SLOB and BLOB plays. Do they go when the referee hands the ball to the inbounds passer or when the passer slaps the ball or calls a signal? The former allows you to preserve what can be a crucial second in avoiding a five-second call. Whichever you prefer, have a rule, and remind players of it, since players can get casual in these situations.

FROM THE DEFENSIVE PERSPECTIVE

Defending BLOB plays often is overlooked, but it is no less important. Take the baseline halfcourt situation. If you are inclined to play man defense, how do you handle the inevitable screens? Do you switch them all, only the screens by the bigs, or something else? Or are you inclined to fight over or go under screens, play straight up defense, and minimize the risk of a mismatch?

Some form of switching screens is advisable. Tracking the ball is more difficult when the ball originates out-of-bounds and under the other team's basket than when the ball is above the foul line and in front of the defense for all to see. In a typical halfcourt offensive set, much of the movement, especially off screens, is away from the basket, while the inbounds situation features players moving off screens directly toward the basket. Any hesitation can be fatal.

It is better to switch everything to match up with every offensive player. While mismatches can occur, the risk that a well-executed screen might spring someone wide open for a second or two close to the basket is greater than the risk a mismatch poses because, in the latter situation, at least a defender is on the ball. This is especially important when the inbounder is a good shooter. Shooters who inbound the ball are almost always an option on the inbounds play, and sometimes the first. Said the late Rick Majerus, "Switch if you have to! It's not the mismatch that beats you. It's the open shot!"

Another way to defend a BLOB play is a 2–3 zone, which increases the predictability of the offense, which against a zone often relies on passes to the top or to the corners, where offensive players can more easily get open. One risk with the zone is handling screens, especially back screens to spring players from the top into zone gaps, which can be dangerous. Furthermore, if you defend the inbounds play with a zone, be sure the team knows whether they should stay in zone the entire possession or revert to man defense at some point, for example, after one or two passes.

A twist on the 2–3 zone is trapping the inbounds passer. Once the referee delivers the ball to the offense, the inbounds passer may not move. Upon ball delivery, consider sending the player positioned in the middle of the zone and the player occupying the strong-side corner to trap the passer. The weak-side corner covers the weak-side block and the interior passing lane, the strong-side guard is responsible for the strong-side corner, and the weak-side guard clogs the lane middle. Most teams do not see this trap regularly. It can unsettle.

SLOB defense is similar. Again, consider switching everything unless you are relatively certain the other team wants only to inbound the ball safely to set up their halfcourt offense. Otherwise, they intend to score, and you must be prepared to deal with screens, including perimeter screens to free up shooters or back screens to set up lobs. Also anticipate reversal of the ball to the inbounds passer for a quick perimeter shot. As noted earlier, identify their best shooters and be alerted if one takes the ball out. In addition, recall the earlier discussion about use of the double-team in late-game situations (see chapter 8).

❂ ❂ ❂

In the end, inbounds plays are about how to round out the team playbook, how much players can absorb, and where to place emphasis. They present opportunities for advantage.

14

PRACTICING SPECIAL SITUATIONS

"They say that nobody is perfect. Then they tell you practice makes perfect. I wish they'd make up their minds."—Wilt Chamberlain

After I retire from coaching, a local high school coach asks me to teach his team a specific defense. I agree, one thing leads to another, and before long I am attending practices and games regularly. I recommend he add situational work to practices. He initially resists. Like most coaches, his hands are full allocating precious practice time among various other prized activities. But when the team shows a tendency to struggle protecting leads late in games, my recommendation elevates to a nag and he allows me to introduce an end-of-the-game drill.

The drill assumes a six-point lead with three minutes left. We vary team fouls; require a minimum number of passes in the half-court sets; limit takes to high-percentage shots; change defenses to mix things up; use timeouts to remind, refocus, and recalibrate; increase offensive rebounding effort; and require use of the jump stop on dribble penetration (among other things). We stop the clock from time to time to repeat possessions to stress certain variables. We score the drill to keep it competitive.

Less than two weeks later, we are in a league game at home, nursing a six-point lead as the game clock approaches three minutes. Déjà vu all over again! We call timeout to remind everyone we are on familiar turf and review the essentials of what must happen to win. The confidence on the players' faces and in their body language is manifest, and we send the boys out to close out the game. Their comfort level on the floor is evident. They mimic most things we covered in the practices and deliver a virtually mistake-free and poised-filled three minutes of basketball. We control the balance of the game and ease into the W.

WHEN COACHING VALUES AND PHILOSOPHY INTERSECT WITH PRACTICES

Here is a universal truth: Finding time for everything a coach wants to cover in practice is impossible. We constantly prioritize practice time, especially as the season advances. What does the team need most to work on *now* to achieve team goals? Should we augment the playbook? Should we concentrate less on conditioning and fundamentals and more on defense and rebounding? Are we spending too much time on transition work and not enough time on foul shooting? What did recent games teach us we need to work on in practice? The list goes on.

Finding practice time, on top of everything else, for anticipated game situations can present a formidable challenge. To state the obvious, practice is geared toward preparing for game performance, and emphasis on special situations is dress rehearsal for the real stage. Why not *regularly* allocate practice time to specific game situations and even film those parts of practice? According to the late Don Meyer, "It is not what you teach, but what you emphasize."

For example, should you work regularly on an end-of-period 2-for-1 set? What about play options for the opening jump ball? Should practices include use of "special teams," for example, for foul-shooting situations, full-court pressure situations, small ball, and particular "stop" possessions? This can be a moving target, as coaches may not know what their team needs until they experience certain situations in games or discern patterns in film.

How often you choose to work on game situations boils down to how much value you place on this component of game preparedness and how willing you are to reconsider old routines. Some coaches spend time on situations once a week, others at the end of each practice, and others still less frequently. Said Jeff Van Gundy, "Your decisions reveal your priorities."

PREPARING A GAME SITUATION PLAN

Consider a preseason coaches' meeting to develop a list that ranks game situations in order of anticipated recurrence, which can form the basis for allocating practice time to specific game situations. As the season goes on, and the team develops its identity and reveals more clearly its strengths and weaknesses, you can reassess and reprioritize practice activities. That list is its own probability framework: The more likely or important a situation, the more time in practice it receives and the better the odds of success for the team.

The list can also form the basis for a master situational practice plan for the season, which forces the coaching staff to think hard about what to emphasize and how to allocate time for special situations. Consider also a special situations planning chart for easy access in games or a list of plays available in games on index cards or in a notebook for specific situations.

Once the list and master plan are developed, ask, "What is the best use of the coaching staff in various game situations, including who is best suited to run situational practice drills?" In other words, identify how each coach can best perform the various roles. Include players. Urge them to think strategically about how to handle situations and encourage them to be vocal in practice to increase their ability to think the game. Increasing basketball IQ throughout the course of a season can easily make a favorable difference in game performance. The more you focus on teaching players to think like coaches, the better their decisions and more effective team play.

Consider also holding an early season team meeting devoted exclusively to game situations. Sell the importance of spending practice time on game situations, which may not always be at the top of player priority lists. While some of what you cover will be hypothetical at that seasonal stage, an early meeting forges a foundational mind-set for down the road. You can also introduce situational game rules at this time, for instance, how to handle loose balls on the floor, who takes the ball out under the basket in certain situations, how to handle the out-of-bounds loose ball, certain "calls" or signals for situations like your 2-for-1 set at the end of a quarter, and what time on the clock triggers your 2-for-1 set (see chapter 4), to name but a handful. (See also appendix D.)

The next section provides a model master plan for practicing situations, primarily using halfcourt and full-court scrimmage structures integrated into daily and weekly drill practice formats. By integrating routine practice formats, the scrimmage structures provide an efficient means to improve game performance without undermining existing practice systems.

DAILY SITUATIONAL WORK IN PRACTICES

Situations are best practiced in conditions that assimilate game reality. For example, an early practice drill on the center jump—before players have worked up a sweat—approximates reality. In contrast, working on an end-of-the-game drill at the start of practice hardly mirrors game conditions.

The halfcourt scrimmage, typically in the form of 5-on-5 offensive and defensive work, is a workable format for practicing certain situations daily or more frequently than once a week. One way is to provide each team rotating possessions; for instance, five consecutive possessions, and make the work competitive in whatever ways work for your team, including rewards for offensive and defensive achievements.

Using the Halfcourt Scrimmage Format

1. *Jump ball.* Starting the half-court scrimmage (and, of course, any full-court scrimmage) with a jump-ball play is easy. The winner of the tip can attack the basket assigned to them, and that half of the floor can become the location for the balance of the halfcourt scrimmage.
2. *Quick hitter.* The quick hitter can be integrated into halfcourt work like any other offensive set but with limited time on the shot clock.
3. *Second-chance opportunities.* Teams in the halfcourt scrimmage can use various offensive rebounding approaches, depending on how the halfcourt work is structured and possessions allocated.

For example, if you give each team five possessions, you can have teams, at their discretion, alternate three to glass, four to glass, or five to glass during the five-possession set. Making this competitive, for example, by rewarding offensive rebounds in some fashion, should raise the quality of play and develop good habits.

4. *SLOB.* Require teams to start some halfcourt possessions at the sideline using one of your SLOB plays.

5. *BLOB.* The same applies here, although you might mix this up by putting limited time on the clock to provide each team the chance to seek a last-second shot on a BLOB play under its own basket. Again, think about making these sessions competitive.

6. *Substitution protocol.* Establish a halfcourt scrimmage substitution protocol that enforces the rules for substitution, as discussed in chapter 3. The same applies to full-court scrimmages. Again, assimilate game conditions. Have substitutions sit on game seats or benches and report to a scorer's table (imaginary or real, as practical).

7. *Fouls-to-give.* Put limited time on the clock (e.g., 20 or fewer seconds) and give each team a specific number of possessions where the defense has two or three fouls to give. The offense can start their possession from the halfcourt sideline. The goal of the defense is to force the offense to use clock and restart their halfcourt plays, and the goal of the offense is to get a good shot within limited time remaining after the last foul is given.

8. *End of quarter.* Place 55 seconds (or a comparable amount) on the clock and have each team run your 2-for-1 set. The offense can bring the ball up from various floor spots, including the opposite baseline. Allow all possessions to play out on both ends of the floor, and make this competitive, with consequences. For the final possession, put 30 seconds (or a comparable amount) on the clock, have both teams in the bonus, and have them try to close out the period with a score or a stop. Give them each a few possessions. You can have teams inbound the ball at the halfcourt sideline.

Transition Drills and Special Situations

Transition work, which most teams do regularly, allows teams to work on special situations. One way is to start a transition sequence with a foul shot and have each team experiment with variations on the make, for instance, the defense can spring a press on the other team or use substitutions to stop the action and slow them down. You can also have the shooting team intentionally miss the foul shot and run a two-point or three-point play (see chapter 2).

Halfcourt Shot

Players like to launch halfcourt shots during dead times in practice. A make yields bragging rights. While this tendency can be a distraction, it also presents an opportunity to accomplish two goals: lighten up practice and practice a shot that occurs at least once, if not more often, each season. Consider this near the end of practice with rewards.

WEEKLY SITUATIONAL WORK IN PRACTICES

The full-court scrimmage is an equally effective format to review other special situations once a week. The trick is to change the variables. Changing the situational assumptions during a full-court scrimmage—a little stop and go—might annoy players, as they can be narrowly focused on "winning" the scrimmage. But the long-term benefits are worth suffering some player angst.

Consider devising a cumulative scoring system for each phase to heighten the competitive nature of the activities. Also, many situations that work in the halfcourt scrimmage work well in the full-court scrimmage format.

Timeouts

Like regular games, scrimmages provide opportunities to use dead-ball time, as well as formal timeouts. The scrimmage is an excellent way to develop the habit of using downtime to advantage. Each team should have a set number of timeouts for the scrimmage and also be primed to use the "free" timeouts (see chapter 1). Assistant coaches should carefully monitor this aspect of the scrimmage. For example:

1. Teams on the floor should assemble during all dead-ball situations, as applicable rules permit.
2. The team, or at least team leadership, should retreat to the bench during the first shot of a shooting foul to caucus with their respective scrimmage coach.
3. Scrimmage coaches should use substitutions to convey information to players on the floor and freeze the ball on an inbounds play after a free throw to allow the substituting team to set up their defense or slow down the other team.
4. Players should adhere to regular timeout protocol.
5. Consider using a timeout to freeze a shooter (see chapter 1).

Begin the Scrimmage at the Start of the Second Half

On occasion, start the scrimmage at halftime with one team up 15 or more points. Assign an assistant to work with each team, one to work on a comeback strategy and the other focused on protecting the lead. Normal rules apply.

Three Minutes Left in the Game

No matter how the scrimmage plays out, at some point during the season—the earlier the better—it is helpful to reset the clock at three (or more) minutes and run each team through end-of-game variables. Alternatively, you can create a separate three-minute drill. In either case, consider the following:

1. Use a game differential of eight to 10 points. While you always can vary the differential, eight to 10 points is a good starting point for finishing games.
2. Vary the foul situations, for example, both teams in the bonus, one team in the bonus, and one team with two fouls to give or both teams with a specified number of fouls to give, or other combinations.

3. For the trailing team, experiment with the following: 1) full-court press either from the start of the three-minute period or at some time soon thereafter, unless they have narrowed the lead significantly after a couple of early possessions; 2) halfcourt traps; 3) a clear understanding of what coaches consider permissible shots; 4) consistently attacking the rim seeking contact; 5) threes only permitted in the designed flow of the offense; and 6) a specific rebound strategy to increase second chances.

4. For the team ahead, experiment with the following: 1) a time management offense, using clock efficiently, valuing the ball, and looking for high-percentage shots; 2) seeking to minimize fouls; and 3) a specific rebound strategy that emphasizes defensive balance and limits second-chance opportunities.

5. At some point, stop the action and have the teams compete in a tie-game situation with one minute left in the game. Again, vary the foul situations.

Final-Possession Situations

You can end scrimmages with this situation, and all of its variations, or segregate it as a distinct drill. There are many scenarios to contemplate, so it is wise to think about which ones will prepare your team best for the unfamiliar. However you parse this, run different score scenarios, for instance, tied game, a one-possession game, and a two-possession game.

Here are other things to keep in mind:

1. In both tied-game and lead situations, the defense should work on its "switch everything" defense or other preferred variations, for example, switching only guards.

2. The team with the lead should work on a keep-away drill, keeping the ball in the hands of their best foul shooters.

3. The team trailing should look to foul early depending on the score or look to trap or steal the ball. If fouling, target weaker foul shooters.

Assorted Situational Scenarios

The more you stress them, the higher the team basketball IQ. Familiarity breeds comfort and confidence.

1. Inbounds play, with less than 10 seconds, under your own basket.
2. Full-court play, with less than 10 seconds, under the other basket.
3. Down one or two, with 10 seconds or less left, and the other team is on the foul line with one shot.
4. Down three, with the ball, and ample time to get off a good shot.
5. Down three, with the ball, and less than 10 seconds on the clock. Defense: Try to foul to eliminate the risk of a three-point goal. Offense: Try to foul to eliminate the risk of a three-point goal.
6. Down four or more, with the ball, with sufficient time to run a halfcourt set.
7. Down three, and defending, with 10 seconds left, and the offense has the ball at the other end of the floor.
8. Down four or more, and defending the final possession.
9. Up two, and defending, with sufficient time for the other team to run a halfcourt set.
10. Up one, two, or three, and defending, with less than five seconds left, and the other team must go the length of the floor.
11. Up two, and defending, with seven seconds left, and other team has the ball sideline out of bounds.
12. Up three, and defending, and with sufficient (but barely enough) time for a three-point attempt.
13. Up three, and defending, with ample time for the other team to get off a good shot.

Purposeful Miss of a Foul Shot

There are five seconds left, with the team on the foul line, with one shot, and you are down two. Seek an immediate shot off the rebound. Change the situation to down three. Seek a three-point shot off a missed foul shot. Consider working on this situation in stages, with the defense cooperating at first to allow the rebound. Later, you can spring the play by surprise in a scrimmage when the foul shooter has two shots, without regard as to whether it is necessary to win.

* * *

There are endless ways to construct a situational basketball practice program. The key is coming to terms with how important you believe it is to devote precious practice time to situations for the short-term and long-term success of your team.

CONCLUSION

Writing this book reminded me constantly that, after so many years spent coaching, I have much to learn about the game we often label "simple," but which endlessly inspires refinements, changes, and new perspectives. Teaching old dogs new tricks is more than a common idiom; it encases a real-life challenge for coaches steeped in routine and time-weathered coaching styles and philosophies.

Beyond the borders of our respective comfort zones, however, lies a bountiful array of exciting new opportunity and experimentation that can be personally rewarding, help us better serve our athletes, and, with renewed vigor, advance the goals of basketball programs. Every now and then, we owe ourselves a fresh perspective on how we do our jobs as coaches to ensure we discharge our responsibilities creatively and in the most effective manner reasonably possible. A fresh look at how to approach situational basketball is precisely the kind of subject that calls on coaches to reassess how to get players ready for game competition. I hope this book challenges you, triggers reflection, and opens new avenues for success.

Appendix A

GAME ASSIGNMENTS FOR COACHING STAFF

Activity	Assistant Coach	Chapter Reference
Tracking timeouts (both teams), monitoring the possession arrow, and reminding players of both	Coach M. Brown	chapter 1
Monitoring whether the other team is about to call a timeout	Coach M. Brown	chapters 1, 8
Ensuring the team assembles during dead-ball situations	Coach Adams	chapter 1
Calling players to the bench during foul shots	Coach Kerr	chapter 1
List of players to foul on the other team	Coach Adams	chapters 2, 7
Making substitutions and monitoring substitutions of the other team	Coach Adams	chapter 3
Speaking to players who come off the floor	Coach M. Brown	chapter 3
Monitoring players for fatigue	all assistants	chapter 3
Monitoring one-dimensional players for team balance	Coach Adams	chapter 3
Alerting referees to the intention to call a timeout after a make or to avoid a five-second call; to foul someone intentionally; to violate the jump ball	Coach Kerr	chapters 7, 8, 11
Reminding players they can run the baseline after a make	Coach M. Brown	chapters 7, 8
Monitoring defensive matchups	Coach Adams	chapter 9

Appendix B

GAME SIGNALS

Game Situation	Signal	Chapter Reference
Pressure when the other team is out of timeouts	blanket	chapter 1
Giving a foul	spade	chapters 2; 4
Fouling strategy to avoid a three-point shot attempt	deuce	chapters 2, 8
Intentionally missing a foul shot	iron	chapters 2, 8
Full-court desperation heave	Montana	chapter 2
Player needs a blow	closed fist	chapter 3
Two-for-one set	double down	chapters 4, 7
Full-court pressure after a make	power	chapters 1, 4; 5
Fouling away from the ball (hack-a-Shaq)	O'Neil	chapters 4, 6
Forcing a shot clock violation	clamp down	chapter 4
Zone defense on a make; man on a miss	Alabama	chapter 5
Contesting an outlet pass or matching up with the outlet receiver	mix	chapter 5
Keeping the ball away from the defense to avoid a foul	gold	chapter 7
Stall or continuity offense	Tar Heel	chapter 7
Switching defenses (guard to guard; big to big; everyone)	palms-up guards (bigs or all)	chapters 7, 8
Going coast to coast off a rebound or a make at the end of a game (or period) without a timeout	Danny Boy	chapter 8
Sending five to the glass	all-hands	chapter 8

Jump-ball violation   scuttle   chapter 11

Appendix C

SPECIALTY LINEUPS AND PLAYER ROLES

Lineup	Name of Player(s)	Chapter Reference
Best long passer	G. Hill	chapter 1
Best foul-shooting team	Nash, Curry, Barry, Price, Stojaković	chapters 2, 5, 7
Platoon group (the "posse")	Havlicek, Cooper, V. Johnson, Starks, Schrempf	chapter 3
Finishing team	Jordan, West, Bryant, Bird, E. Johnson	chapter 3
Best rebounding team	Drummond, Hayes, Rodman, Chamberlin, Russell	chapter 6
Best defensive team	Russell, Pippen, Jones, Iguodala, Frazier	chapters 7, 8
Three-point-shooting team	Curry, K. Thompson, Allen, Kerr, Rice	chapter 7
Best press offensive team	Nash, Anderson, T. Hardaway, I. Thomas, J. Williams	chapter 7
Small-ball team	Curry, Green, Durant, Thompson, Iguodala	chapter 9

Appendix D

SPECIAL GAME RULES

Situation	Rule	Chapter Reference
Coach who may call timeout	head coach only	chapter 1
Players who may call timeout	point guard	chapter 1
Where to gather during timeouts	full: players in game on bench; others around; 30: all on court in circle	chapter 1
When a timeout is permitted to avoid an out-of-bounds call	fourth quarter only	chapter 1
General substitution rules	tucked in shirt; report at scorer's table; wait until referee waves in	chapter 3
Substitution to stop the action during a foul shot	report after the ball is given to the foul shooter on the last shot	chapter 3
Substitution for a player in foul trouble	report before the ball is given to the foul shooter for the first shot of one-and-one and the second shot of a shooting foul	chapter 3
When to initiate the 2-for-1 set	46–50 seconds	chapters 4, 7
End-of-period shots allowed	uncontested layup anytime; otherwise best available shot in eight seconds or less	chapter 4
When to initiate a play on the last possession of a period or game	10–12 seconds	chapters 4, 8
When to take a shot on the last possession of a period or game	5–8 seconds	chapters 4, 8
Bench countdown of the shot or game clock	at 10 seconds	chapter 4
Offensive discipline rules to protect a lead	uncontested layup anytime; best available shot otherwise at 15 seconds or less;	chapter 5

	minimum four to six passes; both sides of the floor gets touches	
End-of-game assignments	who inbounds ball when being pressed; who does so when looking for an end-of-game shot; who should take the final shot of the game	chapter 7
When to foul on a last possession when behind	immediately; after two passes; or no later than five seconds into a possession	chapter 8
Shots allowed when ahead with the last possession	uncontested layup	chapter 8

Appendix E

SITUATIONAL PLAY LIST

As discussed throughout this book, numerous situations exist for which a coach might want a specific play. The volume of available plays and offensive and defensive systems in the marketplace could fill a presidential library. This book does not aspire to augment that bountiful resource. Coaches can easily extract from the existing vast universe of materials what works best for them. To facilitate selection, however, the following is a list of situations discussed earlier for which coaches might want a specific play at the ready, mindful of the limits of what teams can absorb and how coaches prioritize their playbooks.

Counter of an Existing Play to Surprise the Defense (Chapter 1)

To counter an existing play to surprise the defense, you want an available play that "looks" familiar to the defense but is modified enough to surprise them and relatively easy for your team to execute.

Full-Court Play in the Closing Moments of a Game or Period (Chapters 1, 4, 8)

While a full-court play in the last minutes of a game or period can feature a primary ball handler and good finisher going coast to coast à la Danny Ainge, it is a form of transition or secondary offense and can have many options.

Three-Point Shot to Tie or Win a Game (Chapters 2, 8)

Assuming there is limited time on the clock and anticipating a foul, a three-point shot to tie or win a game can be a quick catch-and-shoot or a play off of a screen. If a foul is not anticipated and time permits, you can run something with more movement to increase perimeter options. Consider having two plays or one without multiple options for this situation.

Quick-Hitter (Chapters 4, 8)

Every team needs one or more quick-hitters, especially plays that opponents have not seen. The quick-hitter is particularly useful when little time remains on the shot, period, or game clocks and executing a 2-for-1 set (see the next section).

2-for-1 (Chapter 4)

The challenge in the 2-for-1 is constructing the entire scenario in one set since circumstances vary based on different clock times, different game situations, and how the other team responds. You can conceivably only have enough time at each end for quick-hitters. Or you might have time to use both a quick-hitter and an existing play from your system.

The Last Shot of a Period or Game (Chapters 4, 8)

For the last shot of a period or game, you can use quick-hitters if time is limited. Even if there is more time than needed for a quick-hitter, you can run a weave or other form of continuity to keep the defense moving and the offense in rhythm, and strike when the clock approaches your specified initiation point. Alternatively, you can run something that develops more slowly, so long as you leave the other team little time to implement a play if they get the ball after your possession.

The Time Management Mode (Chapter 7)

What you select when in time management mode may depend on whether you play in a shot clock system. In either case, however, a continuity or motion offense can be effective, provided your team has the discipline to execute and stay true to the design. A motion offense forces a defense to work hard, creates possibilities, can be unpredictable, and can yield high-percentage shots.

Reset When the Called Play for a Last Shot of the Game Is Foiled (Chapter 8)

When a called play to close out a period or game goes awry, entrusting the team to freelance to arrive at a solution can be a leap of faith. On the other hand, a team that can adjust on the fly is manna for any coaching staff. But in case you are not blessed with take-charge athletes when things get tough, consider having a simple play available you can call from the bench. This can be a pick-and-roll, pop, or isolation for a specific player to operate.

"Keep Away" When the Other Team Is Trying to Foul and Stop the Clock (Chapter 8)

Playing "keep away" when the other team is trying to foul or stop the clock can be a variation of a motion offense, although using the old University of North Carolina four corners offense can also be effective. As discussed, the other team will not allow you to keep the ball for too long, but if players are well trained, you can obtain some extra seconds.

Out-of-Bounds Play Under Your Own Basket with Less Than 10 Seconds on the Clock (Chapters 8, 13)

As discussed, depending on the precise number of seconds involved, with an out-of-bounds play under your own basket, you are looking at a quick-hitter or relatively quick-developing play with limited passing and dribbling. The alternative to having two plays is a multioption single play that covers both scenarios: a quick-hitter with immediate second and third options.

Out of Bounds Under the Opposition Basket with Less Than 10 Seconds on the Clock (Chapters 4, 8, 13)

The options when out of bounds under the opposition's basket are whether to have your team travel the length of the floor (chapters 4, 8) or a use a half-court sideline out-of-bounds play after moving the ball to half court and taking a timeout (chapter 13). Consider having the former in your playbook regardless, since you eventually might be in a situation where that is the only option (when no timeouts are left) or is the best option (for whatever reason).

A Play for After the Purposefully Missed Foul Shot (Chapter 8)

If you only need two points and the execution of the missed foul shot works well enough, you likely will not need a play, as whoever gets the ball should have a decent shot available. If you need three points, however, you will need something specific off the offensive rebound that includes primary and secondary three-point-shooter options.

Inbounds Play to Get the Ball to the Best Foul Shooter (Chapters 8, 13)

When the other team is giving fouls to stop the clock and extend the game, the goal is to get the ball to your best foul shooter off an inbounds play. Because the other team might double-team your intended pass receiver, you need a second option.

Jump-Ball Attack Play (Chapter 11)

The text includes one such jump-ball play; others can be found or designed anew. Again, this is a recurring situation coaches can exploit.

Inbounds Play to Score Off a Quick-Hitter at the Rim (Chapter 13)

The approach on an inbounds play to score off a quick-hitter at the rim is to devise a relatively quick play that uses screens and cuts to cause the defense to lose sight of one player cutting to the basket.

Inbounds Play with Multiple Options (Chapter 13)

An inbounds play with multiple options is a form of motion offense that has all five players, including the inbounds entry passer after the pass, moving off screens and making cuts. Because defenders are not set up in typical roles and spaces on the floor, they have to make quick decisions in an unfamiliar situation. Players should be free to make an opportunistic play off the designed set.

Inbounds Play to Get the Ball Safely to a Guard to Start the Offense (Chapter 13)

An inbounds play to get the ball safely to a guard to start the offense is relatively straightforward. A screen or two to spring the point guard free usually will suffice. Have a second option in case the intended pass receiver cannot get open.

Inbounds Play to Get a Quick Three-Point Shot (Chapters 8 and 13)

An inbounds play to get a quick three-point shot can come in handy during crunch time or to surprise the defense. If time permits, run something with more than a single-shooter option. A three-point goal off a designed inbounds play can provide a boost and unsettle the opposition.

Appendix F

POSSESSIONS CHART

Unless your staff includes a math whiz who can execute quick calculations under pressure, or even if it does, you might find a cheat sheet helpful as a reminder of how many possessions likely remain at certain points of the game. Of course, the number of possessions cannot always be predicted with precision because each game has a life of its own. Quick scores and turnovers or long defensive stands will alter the math. A general guide, however, is a useful benchmark for decision making in situations where time is a diminishing asset.

Minutes (Seconds) Remaining	Presumed Minimum Possessions Remaining in the Game (Both Teams Combined) (Based on 35-Second Shot Clock)	Presumed Maximum Possessions Remaining in the Game (Both Teams Combined) (Based on Average Possession of 23 Seconds)
4:00 (240 seconds)	7	11
3:00 (180 seconds)	6	8
2:30 (150 seconds)	5	7
2:00 (120 seconds)	4	6
1:40 (100 seconds)	3	5
1:20 (80 seconds)	3	4
1:00 (60 seconds)	2	3
50 seconds	2	3
40 seconds	2	2

ADDITIONAL RESOURCES

Websites

Basketball HQ, http://www.basketballhq.com
Breakthrough Basketball, http://www.breakthroughbasketball.com
Coaches Clipboard, http://www.coachesclipboard.net
Hoops Skills, http://www.hoopskills.com
Hoop Tactics, http://hooptactics.com
Stronger Team, http://www.strongerteam.com

Books

The Adjustable Area Man-to-Man Press, by Burral Paye
Basketball: Multiple Offense and Defense, by Dean Smith
Basketball Defense: Lessons from the Legends, by Jerry Krause and Ralph Pim
Basketball Offense: Lessons from the Legends, by Jerry Krause and Ralph Pim
Basketball Playbook 2, by Bob Ociepka and Dale Raterman
Basketball Tip-Ins (100 Tips and Drills for Young Basketball Players), by Nick Sortal
Blackboard Strategies: Over 200 Favorite Plays from Successful Coaches for Nearly Every Possible Situation, by Eric Sacharski
Coaching Basketball Successfully, by Morgan Wootten and Dave Gilbert
Free Throw: 7 Steps to Success at the Foul Line, by Dr. Tom Ambeerry
NBA Coaches Playbook: Techniques, Tactics, and Teaching Points, by the National Basketball Coaches Association and edited by Giorgio Gandolfi
Stuff Good Players Should Know, by Dick Devenzio
A System of Game Execution: Observations of Ralph Miller's Pressure Basketball, by Steve Seidler
Wooden on Leadership: How to Create a Winning Organization, by John Wooden and Steve Jamison

YouTube

End of Basketball Situations (MacKey), https://www.youtube.com/watch?v=7M1ws1mqegY
Special Situations (Mike Longabardi), https://www.youtube.com/watch?v=PhBPj9reGSg

Special Situations in Basketball (John Dore), https://www.youtube.com/watch?v=uIZygRjzZA8

Special Situations in Offense (Brian Hill), https://www.youtube.com/watch?v=kOg79W2-SMg

DVDs and VHS

The Blizzard Match-Up Zone Defense (Joe McKeown)
Championship Practices (Duke Basketball Video Series)
Over 50 Game-Winning Last-Second Plays
Planning and Executing Special Situations (Mike Fratello)
Practice Planning and Drills for Mental Toughness (Bob Knight)
Winning Close Games with Special Plays (Bob McKillop)

INDEX

ABOUT THE AUTHOR

Michael Coffino, prior to launching his writing career, was a litigation and international attorney for 36 years, and a youth and high school basketball coach for 24 years. He is coauthor, with Joan Barnes, founder of Gymboree, of a memoir entitled *Play It Forward: From Gymboree to the Yoga Mat and Beyond* (2016). Coffino has also completed a handbook for high school basketball coaches, planned for release in 2017, and is working on a book about high school athletics, as well as two other memoirs, one a life story and another about a professional basketball player and coach. A black belt in karate and guitar player, he was born and raised in the Bronx (Highbridge), New York. He lives in Tiburon, California (Marin County), and has two adult children living in San Francisco.